YOU CAN
YOU WILL
Journal

Also by Joel Osteen

Break Out!
Break Out! Journal
Daily Readings from Break Out!
I Declare
I Declare Personal Application Guide
Every Day a Friday
Every Day a Friday Journal
Daily Readings from Every Day a Friday
You Can, You Will
Your Best Life Now
Daily Readings from Your Best Life Now
Starting Your Best Life Now
Your Best Life Now Study Guide
Your Best Life Now for Moms
Your Best Life Begins Each Morning
Your Best Life Now Journal

YOU CAN
YOU WILL
Journal

A Guide to Developing the
8 Undeniable Qualities *of a* **WINNER**

JOEL OSTEEN

Faith
Words

New York • Boston • Nashville

Unless otherwise indicated, all Scripture quotations are taken from *The Holy Bible, New International Version®* NIV®. Copyright © 1973, 1978, 1984, 2011 by Biblica, Inc.™ Used by permission. All rights reserved worldwide.

Scripture quotations noted NLT are taken from the *Holy Bible, New Living Translation*, copyright © 1996, 2004, 2007 by Tyndale House Foundation. Used by permission of Tyndale House Publishers, Inc., Carol Stream, Illinois 60188. All rights reserved.

Scripture quotations noted NKJV are taken from the *New King James Version* of the Bible. Copyright © 1982 by Thomas Nelson, Inc. Used by permission. All rights reserved.

Scripture quotations noted AMP are from *The Amplified Bible*. Copyright © 1954, 1958, 1962, 1964, 1965, 1987 by The Lockman Foundation. All rights reserved. Used by permission. (www.Lockman.org)

Scripture quotations noted KJV are from the *King James Version* of the Holy Bible.

Scriptures noted MSG are from *The Message*. Copyright © 1993, 1994, 1995, 1996, 2000, 2001, 2002. Used by permission of NavPress Publishing Group.

Literary development and design: Koechel Peterson & Associates, Inc., Minneapolis, Minnesota.

This book has been adapted from *You Can, You Will*, copyright © 2014 by Joel Osteen. Published by FaithWords.

FaithWords
Hachette Book Group
1290 Avenue of the Americas
New York, NY 10104
www.faithwords.com

Printed in the United States of America

First Edition: March 2015

10 9 8 7 6 5 4 3 2 1

FaithWords is a division of Hachette Book Group, Inc. The FaithWords name and logo are trademarks of Hachette Book Group, Inc.

The Hachette Speakers Bureau provides a wide range of authors for speaking events. To find out more, go to www.hachettespeakersbureau.com or call (866) 376-6591.

The publisher is not responsible for websites (or their content) that are not owned by the publisher.

ISBN: 978-1-4555-6052-3

CONTENTS

Introduction

If you are like most of us, you believe there is a winner inside of you, but too often we talk ourselves out of God's best. We allow doubts, fears, and the discouraging things people have said to limit us and convince us to settle where we are. Negative voices always speak the loudest.

The truth is that you were created to be successful, to accomplish your goals, to leave your mark on this generation. You have greatness in you. The key is to get it out.

That is why I wrote my book *You Can, You Will*, which provides eight undeniable qualities of a winner and the encouragement that will help you reach your potential so that you can become all you were created to be. I've seen them work in my own life and in the lives of many others.

No matter where you are or what challenges you are facing, you have what it takes to win. You're talented enough. You're smart enough. You're experienced enough. You have the right personality and the right looks. You're the right nationality. You didn't get shortchanged. You're not lacking. You're fully equipped. You're the man or woman for the job.

This journal companion for the book offers that same encouragement in daily doses supplemented by inspirational and thought-provoking material. You will find a wealth of scriptures, inspirational quotations, selected stories, prayers, and points for contemplation. All are provided to engage you in a process of reflection that will enhance your faith and lead you to positive actions.

I am delighted in your interest in this book. It shows that you want to put your faith into action and reach the highest level of your destiny, and God loves that. You'll learn eight powerful keys for your life that will help take you there: keep your vision in front of you, run your race, expect good things, have a positive mind-set, commit to excellence, keep growing, serve others, and stay passionate.

This journal is an open door to self-discovery, so step through and begin the journey toward living the life you were born to live. My prayer is that you will take some time each day to read the entries and to add your own thoughts. But don't rush through it. Slow yourself down and take the time to reflect on your life. Let the scriptures speak to your heart. If you are facing challenges or barriers, there are prayers and inspirational quotes to help remind you that God is with you each and every moment. Be still and listen to what God is saying through these words, then put words to your responses.

This is a journal to record life lessons that you don't want to forget. It could be the start to a brand-new beginning for you. Underline important ideas within these pages, write yourself notes of encouragement in the margins as you read, and jot down fresh ideas that come to you as you read. Especially seek God's help and guidance regarding areas in which He may want to change you. It's a reflection of your life journey. What you record you remember. You will discover that it will bring clarity to what God has done, is doing, and wants to do in your life.

Journaling has also been shown to improve problem-solving abilities. Many people find that using a journal helps them to better assess their thoughts and feelings and to find clarity. The process of putting pen to paper and then seeing your words on the page can help you solve problems while keeping matters in perspective and priorities straight. You may release pent-up emotions in the process, and that is a good thing, too.

Be as honest as possible as you write your responses. Don't be afraid to freely express your thoughts and feelings. Don't worry about punctuation, spelling, or grammar when making your own entries. You won't be graded on this.

This journal is designed to provide you twenty-four days of daily inspiration and encouragement in your walk of faith. It is best to read day to day in a quiet place where you can meditate and contemplate for brief periods, away from the usual distractions. Take your time and enter your thoughts and encouragements. Once you've gone through it, feel free to begin again. Replenish your spirit and listen for the still, small voice of God's grace and direction.

Let this journal serve as a record of your daily progress and your entries as a testimony of your faith. Enjoy the process. This is your time. This is your moment. Winning is in your DNA, and it's about to come out in a greater way. You may have had some victories in the past, but you haven't seen anything yet.

As you put these principles on the eight qualities into action, you will step into a new level of your destiny. You will discover talents you didn't know you had, and you will see God's blessing and favor in amazing ways.

Get ready! You can! You will!

KEEP YOUR VISION IN FRONT OF YOU

CHAPTER 1

God Will Finish What He Started

Key Truth

You may not be reaching your highest potential, not because you don't have the faith, the talent, or the determination, but because you're not keeping the right things in front of you.

A young man dreamed of being an actor, but in the early 1980s, he wasn't getting the big parts he wanted. Broke and discouraged, he drove his beat-up old car to the top of a hill overlooking the city of Los Angeles and did something unusual. He wrote himself a check for ten million dollars for "Acting services rendered."

This young man had grown up so poor that his family lived in a Volkswagen van at one time. He put that check in his wallet and kept it there. When things got tough, he'd pull it out and look at it to remind himself of his dream. A dozen years later, that same young man, the comedian Jim Carrey, was making fifteen million to twenty-five million a movie.

Studies tell us that we move toward what we consistently see. You should keep something in front of you, even if it's symbolic, to remind you of what you are believing for.

In the Scripture, Zerubbabel wanted to rebuild the temple. He laid the foundation, but then the people came against him and made him stop. For ten years no work was done. One day the prophet Zechariah came by and told him to do something interesting. He said, "Go get the headstone." The headstone was the stone reserved to be the last piece of stone that went into the building. It was symbolic. It represented the finished product.

Why was it important for Zerubbabel to keep the headstone in front of him? Because every time he looked at the headstone, it was a reminder that God would finish what He started. When Zerubbabel was discouraged, when he was tired and thought it was impossible to finish the job, he would go over and look at the headstone. That was God saying to him, "I'm in control. I'm going to bring it to pass. Just stay in faith."

Let me ask you: Do you have your headstone in front of you? Do you have something that represents the final piece to your dreams?

I learned this from my father. He and my mother started Lakewood Church in 1959, in an old rundown feed store. They had ninety people. You know what my father called the church? Lakewood International Outreach Center.

There was a big blue sign outside. The sign cost more than the building. The truth is, they were a small neighborhood church, but every time my father drove up to that church and saw the sign, his vision was being increased. He was moving toward it.

When the ninety members saw the sign week after week, something was being birthed on the inside. Seeds of increase were taking root. At the old church my father put up a big world map on the wall. He put a globe behind him when he spoke. He always had the world on his mind. One year at a conference, people came from 150 countries. It looked like the United Nations.

Do you know what Lakewood is today? It is an international outreach center touching the world. What you keep in front of you, you're moving toward.

Consider This

———— • ————

When people don't have anything that reminds
them of what they're dreaming about, they get stuck
and lose their passion. Do you have something
you see every day that reminds you of what you're
believing for, something that inspires you, ignites
your faith? Describe what you will put in front of
you to keep your dream in front of you.

....
....
....
....
....
....
....
....
....
....
....
....
....
....
....
....
....
....

What the Scriptures Say

———————◆———————

Where there is no vision, the people perish.

Proverbs 29:18 KJV

And I am convinced and sure of this very thing, that He Who
began a good work in you will continue until the day of Jesus
Christ [right up to the time of His return], developing [that good
work] and perfecting and bringing it to full completion in you.

Philippians 1:6 AMP

....
....
....
....
....
....
....
....
....
....
....
....
....
....
....
....
....
....

Thoughts for Today

Dream lofty dreams, and as you dream, so shall you become.
Your vision is the promise of what you shall one day be.

James Allen

Fires can't be made with dead embers, nor can enthusiasm be
stirred by spiritless men. Enthusiasm in our daily work lightens
effort and turns even labor into pleasant tasks.

James Mark Baldwin

God has great things in store for His people;
they ought to have large expectations.

C. H. Spurgeon

....

....

....

....

....

....

....

....

....

....

....

....

....

....

....

A Prayer for Today

Father in Heaven, this word is for me today. Thank You that I have the assurance that the work You have started to do in my life will be brought to completion by Your love and power. I can and will become everything You created me to be. Help me to keep the vision in front of me and to know that You are bringing my dreams to pass. My hopes and dreams are in Your hands. I trust You.

TAKEAWAY TRUTH

Keep your vision in front of you. All over your house, you should have pictures that inspire you, Scripture verses that encourage you, mementoes that strengthen your faith. Every time you see that reminder of your dream, say under your breath: "Thank You, Lord, for bringing my dreams to pass. Thank You, Lord, that I'll become everything You created me to be." What you keep in front of you, you're moving toward.

CHAPTER 2
God Will Supersize Your Vision

Key Truth

If you keep the vision in front of you and not get talked out of it, but just keep honoring God, being your best, thanking Him that it's on the way, God will supersize whatever you're believing for. He'll do exceedingly abundantly above and beyond.

Now, don't have just a little vision. You're not inconveniencing God to believe big. In fact, it's just the opposite. When you believe to do great things, when you believe to set a new standard for your family, it pleases God.

Take the limits off and say, "I don't see a way, but God, I know You have a way, so I'm going to believe to have children. I will believe to start a business to impact the world. I will believe that my whole family will serve you. I will believe to get totally well."

It doesn't matter what it looks like in the natural; God is a supernatural God. He's not limited by your resources, by your environment, by your education, by your nationality. If you'll have a big vision, God will not only do what you're dreaming about, He will do more than you can ask or think.

A few years after my father went to be with the Lord and I stepped up to pastor the church, I had a desire to write a book. My dad had written many books, and they were all translated into Spanish. On the bookshelf I walk by at home every day, I had two copies of my dad's most popular book. One was in English. The other was in Spanish. I kept those books in front of me, knowing one day at the right time I would write a book. My dream was that it, too, would be translated into Spanish.

In my mind this seemed so far out. I never thought I could get up and minister, much less write a book. This was stretching my faith. A year went by, no book. Two years, three years, four years. It would have been easy to lose my passion and think it was never going to happen. But I had my father's books strategically placed on this bookshelf right outside my closet. I saw them thousands and thousands of times. I didn't always consciously think about them, but even subconsciously I was moving toward writing my own. My faith was being released. Something on the inside was saying, "Yes, one day I'm going to write a book."

In 2004 I wrote my first book, *Your Best Life Now*. When the publisher read the manuscript, they decided to publish it in English and Spanish at the same time. Normally they wait to see if anybody buys it in English. But that's the way God is. His dream for your life is bigger than your own.

I've found that whatever your vision is, God will supersize it. He will do more than you can ask or think. My vision was that my book would be so well received that it would be translated into Spanish. But it was also translated into French, German, Russian, Swahili, Portuguese, and more than forty other languages.

God will supersize whatever you're believing for.

Consider This

You won't be the winner God wants you to be
with small dreams. Your destiny is too great, your
assignment too important, to have little goals and
little prayers. What is the big vision that God
wants you to believe Him for?

What the Scriptures Say

———•———

Now to Him who is able to do exceedingly abundantly
above all that we ask or think, according to the power that works
in us, to Him be glory in the church by Christ Jesus to all
generations, forever and ever. Amen.

Ephesians 3:20–21 NKJV

. . . we're never left feeling shortchanged. Quite the contrary—
we can't round up enough containers to hold everything God
generously pours into our lives through the Holy Spirit!

Romans 5:5 MSG

....
....
....
....
....
....
....
....
....
....
....
....
....
....
....
....
....
....

Thoughts for Today

Vision is the art of seeing things invisible.
Jonathan Swift

Faith, mighty faith, the promise sees and looks to God alone.
Laughs at impossibilities, and cries, "It shall be done."
Charles Wesley

Faith is daring the soul to go beyond what the eyes can see.
William Newton Clark

....
....
....
....
....
....
....
....
....
....
....
....
....
....
....
....
....
....

A Prayer for Today

Father, thank You that You give me not just exceedingly, not just abundantly, but exceedingly abundantly above all I can ask or think. Help me to keep growing in the revelation of Your love and to be bold to ask big and think big. I believe that You have amazing plans for my life and that nothing is impossible with You. Amen.

TAKEAWAY
TRUTH

Don't stop believing. Every time you see your vision, you're moving toward it. Thank God that it's on the way. If you'll do this, God will supersize what you're dreaming about. He will take you further faster, opening doors that no man can shut, doing what no man can do.

CHAPTER 3
Use the Power of Your Imagination

Key Truth

When you keep your vision in front of you, that's your faith being released. If you can see what God has put in your heart, you will receive the incredible things God wants to do.

I know some things do seem far out or very unlikely, but don't ever say: "I can't imagine that." If you see somebody really fit and energetic when you're trying to get back in shape, you may think: "I can't imagine looking like that." You may drive by a nice house and say, "I can't imagine living in this neighborhood." Or you may have thought: "I can't imagine owning my own business." "I can't imagine being that successful."

The problem is you're being limited by your own imagination. You've got to change what you're seeing. Don't let negative thoughts paint those pictures. Use your imagination to see yourself accomplishing dreams, rising higher, overcoming obstacles, being healthy, strong, blessed, and prosperous.

In the Scriptures, God promised Abraham that he would be the father of many nations. In the natural it was impossible. Abraham didn't have one child. He was eighty years old. But God didn't just give him the promise; God gave him a picture to look at.

God said, "Abraham, go out and look at the stars—that's how many descendants you will have." I've read that there are six thousand stars in the Eastern sky where he was. It's not a coincidence that there are six thousand promises in the Scriptures. God was saying, "Every promise that you can get a vision for, I will bring it to pass."

God told him also to look at the grains of sand at the seashore, because that was how many relatives he would have. Why did God give him pictures? God knew there would be times when it would look as if the promise would not come to pass, and Abraham would be discouraged and tempted to give up.

In those times, Abraham would go out at night and look up at the sky. When he saw the stars, faith would rise in his heart. Something would tell him, "It's going to happen. I can see it."

In the morning when his thoughts told him, "You're too old, it's too late, you heard God wrong," he would go down to the beach and look at the grains of sand. His faith would be restored.

Like Abraham, there will be times when it seems as if your dreams are not coming to pass. It's taking so long. The medical report doesn't look good. You don't have the resources. Business is slow. You could easily give up.

But like Abraham, you've got to go back to that picture. Keep that vision in front of you. When you see the key to your new house, the outfit for your baby, the tennis shoes for when you're healthy, the picture frame for your spouse, those pictures of what you're dreaming about will keep you encouraged.

God is saying to you what He said to Abraham: "If you can see it, I can do it. If you have a vision for it, I can make a way. I can open up new doors. I can bring the right people. I can give you the finances. I can break the chains holding you back."

Consider This

You may have struggled with your weight,
your health, your finances, with a relationship, for a
long time and you keep wondering, "Will this ever
change?" God is saying, "You can. You will!" What
is the vision you are believing God will accomplish
in your life? What will you keep in front of
you that declares it will happen?

What the Scriptures Say

———————•———————

Abram said, "Sovereign LORD, what can you give me since I
remain childless and the one who will inherit my estate is Eliezer
of Damascus?" And Abram said, "You have given me no children;
so a servant in my household will be my heir." Then the word of
the LORD came to him: "This man will not be your heir, but a
son who is your own flesh and blood will be your heir." He took
him outside and said, "Look up at the sky and count the stars—
if indeed you can count them." Then he said to him, "So shall
your offspring be." Abram believed the LORD, and
he credited it to him as righteousness.

Genesis 15:2–6

Jesus looked at them and said, "With man this is impossible,
but with God all things are possible."

Matthew 19:26

....
....
....
....
....
....
....
....
....
....
....
....
....
....

Thoughts for Today

The faith of Christ offers no buttons to push for quick service.
The new order must wait the Lord's own time, and that is too
much for the man in a hurry. He just gives up and
becomes interested in something else.

A. W. Tozer

Beware in your prayer, above everything,
of limiting God, not only by unbelief, but by fancying
that you know what He can do.

Andrew Murray

Faith sees the invisible, believes the unbelievable,
and receives the impossible.

Corrie ten Boom

. . . .
. . . .
. . . .
. . . .
. . . .
. . . .
. . . .
. . . .
. . . .
. . . .
. . . .
. . . .
. . . .

A Prayer for Today

Father, You are the all-powerful sovereign Lord of the universe. My dreams are not too big and the challenges in my life are not too difficult. You have a way to bring them to pass. You will do something big in my life. You will release Your favor in a new way. I believe that what You have spoken over my life You will bring to pass, and that what You have promised You will do.

....

....

....

....

....

....

....

....

....

....

....

....

....

....

....

....

....

TAKEAWAY TRUTH

You may think it's too late—your dreams are
too big, your obstacles too difficult—but
God is still on the throne. What you thought
was over and done is still going to happen.
When it looks impossible, God will suddenly
cause things to fall into place, giving you
favor, influence, and connections. I believe
and declare that every dream, every promise,
every goal God put in your heart,
He will bring to pass.

RUN YOUR RACE

CHAPTER 4
Be True to Who God Wants You to Be

Key Truth

If you're going to become the winner you were created to be, you need to be bold. The second quality of a winner is that you run your race the way you want to run it. You should be the original God created you to be.

I read an interesting report from a nurse who takes care of people who are close to death. She asked hundreds of patients facing death what their biggest regrets were. The number one regret was: "I wish I had been true to who I was and not just lived to meet the expectations of others."

How many people today are not being true to who they are because they're afraid they may disappoint someone, they may fall out of their good graces, or they may not be accepted? I say this respectfully, but you can't live the life God wanted for you if you are trying to be who your parents want you to be, who your friends want you to be, or who your boss wants you to be. You have to be true to who God made you to be.

There will always be people who try to squeeze you into their molds and pressure you into being who they want you to be. They may be good people. They may mean well, but the problem is they didn't breathe life into you. They didn't equip you or empower you. God did.

You can't be insecure and you can't worry about what everyone thinks. You can't try to keep everyone happy. If you change with every criticism and play up to people, trying to win their favor, you'll go through life letting people manipulate you and pressure you into their boxes.

You have to accept the fact that you can't keep everyone happy. You can't make everyone like you. You will never win over every critic. Even if you changed and did everything they asked, some would still find fault. You're not really free until you're free from trying to please everyone. You're respectful, you're kind, but you're not living to please people; you're living to please God.

The Scriptures talk about those who loved the praise of people more than the praise of God. One of the tests we all have to pass is when someone in our lives that we respect and look up to—a boss, a friend, a colleague, a relative—wants us to go one direction, when we know in our hearts that we should take another path.

We don't want to hurt their feelings. We don't want to lose their friendship. We want their approval. But if we are to fulfill our destinies, we have to be strong. We have to have this attitude: "I want the praise of God more than the praise of people. I have an assignment. I have a purpose. I will become who God created me to be."

Every morning when you get up, you should search your heart. Know deep down that you're being true to who God called you to be. Then you won't have to look to the left or to the right. Just stay focused on your goals.

Consider This

———•———

God doesn't want you to be an imitation of someone
else. In what ways do you sense that you have been
allowing others to squeeze you into their molds?
What action can you take today to change that?

....
....
....
....
....
....
....
....
....
....
....
....
....
....
....
....
....

What the Scriptures Say

And do not be conformed to this world, but be transformed by the renewing of your mind, that you may prove what is that good and acceptable and perfect will of God.

Romans 12:2 NKJV

". . . for they loved human praise more than praise from God."

John 12:43

Thoughts for Today

Risk! Risk anything! Care no more for the opinions of others, for those voices. Do the hardest thing on earth for you. Act for yourself. Face the truth.

Katherine Mansfield

I am only one, but I am one. I can't do everything, but I can do something. And what I can do, that I ought to do. And what I ought to do, by the grace of God, I will do.

Edward Everett Hale

A Prayer for Today

Father, thank You that You called me to be the person You want and made me to be. I want my life to be fully pleasing to You, and I ask You to transform me through the renewing of my mind so that I will know and be able to walk in Your will and ways. I believe that Your anointing and empowerment and favor will rest upon my life so that I can fulfill Your purpose for me in my generation.

TAKEAWAY TRUTH

Run your own race. Don't look to the left or to the right. Don't try to compete with anyone else. Don't let people control you and go around feeling guilty because you don't fit into their boxes. Don't get upset because something negative is said about you. Look straight ahead and, as the apostle Paul said, run with purpose in every step.

CHAPTER 5
Take Control of Your Happiness

Key Truth

If you allow it, people will run your life. They'll tell you what to do, where to go, how to dress, and how to spend your money. One of life's greatest freedoms is to get free from controlling people.

Too many people sacrifice their own happiness to keep someone else happy. They've got to stop by their friend's house and say hello, because they don't want to upset the friend. They stay late at the office, because if they don't, their boss may be unhappy. They've got to loan this friend money, because the friend is in trouble again. If they don't meet all the demands and fix this person, rescue this person, solve this person's problem, then they'll fall out of somebody's good grace, and that somebody will get upset.

You may feel that if you don't meet all their demands and needs, if you don't rescue them or loan them money, then they'll be angry with you. But if that's the case, maybe it's time for them to be unhappy instead of you. If they get mad, they're manipulators. They are using you.

Your time is too valuable to go through life letting people control you and make you feel guilty if you don't come running every time they call. The easy thing is to just give in and keep bailing them out, so you don't make any waves.

But as long as you rescue them and you're there to cheer them up and keep them all fixed up, you're not really helping them. You're a crutch. Because of you, they don't have to deal with the real issues. You're enabling their dysfunction.

The only way these dependent people will get the help they need is for you to stop being their crutch. Don't come running every time they have an "emergency."

Put your foot down and say, "I love you, but I'm not going to let you control me. I love you, but I'm not jumping every time you call. I love you, but I refuse to feel guilty if I don't meet all your demands."

If people are controlling you, it's not their fault; it's your fault. You have to set some boundaries. Quit allowing them to call you all hours of the day to dump their problems on you. That's why we have voice mail!

Quit caving in to them every time they throw a fit. Ignore it. Quit loaning them money every time they make poor choices. Don't take on a false sense of responsibility. You are not the savior of the world. We already have a Savior. You're not supposed to keep everyone happy or fixed. If you take on that job, the one person who will not be happy is you.

Are you doing too much for other people and not enough for yourself? Are you so good-hearted that you're sacrificing your happiness to keep everyone around you happy? Understand this: Your first priority is to keep yourself happy.

The best thing you can do is to cut the puppet strings. You don't have time to play games, get entangled, or become distracted trying to keep everybody happy. You have a destiny to fulfill. Be bold, take charge of your life, and pursue the dreams God has placed in your heart.

Consider This

———— • ————

Are there people in your life who know
if they pull one string you'll feel guilty, or another
string and you'll bail them out, or another and
you'll stay late and do a work or school project
for them? Describe how people pull your strings.
Define how you will cut those strings.

....
....
....
....
....
....
....
....
....
....
....
....
....
....
....
....
....
....

What the Scriptures Say

---◆---

Am I now trying to win the approval of human beings,
or of God? Or am I trying to please people? If I were still trying
to please people, I would not be a servant of Christ.

Galatians 1:10

The fear of human opinion disables; trusting in
God protects you from that.

Proverbs 29:25 MSG

. . . .
. . . .
. . . .
. . . .
. . . .
. . . .
. . . .
. . . .
. . . .
. . . .
. . . .
. . . .
. . . .
. . . .
. . . .
. . . .

Thoughts for Today

Don't seek to be a people pleaser . . .
don't compromise what you know is right in your heart
to gain the approval of others. The only approval
you need is God's, and you already have that.

Joyce Meyer

Opinions are not facts. Stop worrying about
what people think of you.

Author Unknown

Approval addiction is essentially an act of self-abandonment.
Instead of finding your value and worth from your Creator,
you have given your heart up for adoption. You have given it
away to others for love and approval, making them responsible
for your feelings. . . . Depending on anyone other than God
for fundamental validation is just asking for heartbreak.

Pete Wilson

....
....
....
....
....
....
....
....
....
....
....

A Prayer for Today

Father, thank You that You did not make me
to be other people's puppet and try to please them by
fulfilling their wishes and demands. I want to be loving
and kind and help others who are in real need, but help
me to cut the strings of those who would manipulate me
and use me to their own advantage. I believe that You have
given me a destiny to fulfill and that I will discover true
happiness as I pursue running my own life race.
In Jesus' Name. Amen.

TAKEAWAY TRUTH

Take responsibility for your own happiness. Quit letting others pressure you into being something that you're not. Quit living on eggshells because you don't want to fall out of their favor and get them upset. Let them be upset. If you spend your life trying to please everyone and letting them control you, they may be happy but you'll end up missing your destiny. I'd rather please God and have some people upset with me than please people and have God upset with me.

CHAPTER 6
Fly with Those Who Lift You Up

Key Truth

If you want to reach your highest potential, you need to evaluate the people you're spending time with. You won't lift off or thrust forward into the good things God has in store if you let people dump their loads and negativity on you.

A pilot friend of mine told me there are four main principles to master when flying airplanes: lift, thrust, weight, and drag. You have to take all these into account to make sure the plane will fly.

It struck me that these same principles apply to specific types of people. There are some who lift you, brighten your day, cheer you up, and make you feel better about yourself. They're a lift. Then there are people who thrust you. They inspire you, motivate you, and challenge you to move forward and pursue your dreams. The people in the third group are weights. They pull you down, dump their problems on you, so that you leave feeling heavier, negative, discouraged, and worse than you did before. Finally, there are those who are a drag. They've always got a sad song. The dishwasher broke. They didn't get invited to a party. They're stuck in a pit. They expect you to cheer them up, fix their problems, and carry their loads.

We all encounter people from each of these four groups. You have to make sure you're spending the majority of your time with lifters and thrusters. If you're only hanging out with weights and drags, it will keep you from becoming everything you were created to be.

If you expect to reach your highest potential, you need to evaluate the people with whom you're spending time. You won't lift off or thrust forward into the good things God has in store if you're weighted down, letting people dump their loads on you. They'll make you discouraged and drain your energy. You're not responsible for their happiness. Sure, there are times when we need to sow a seed and have a listening ear and take time to love people back into wholeness. But that should be for a season and not an ongoing drama.

You need to be around lifters and thrusters—people who inspire you and motivate you. To do that, you may have to make changes in whom you spend time with and whose phone calls you take. You shouldn't spend an hour on the phone every night listening to somebody's woes or hearing their sad songs. Put an end to it. Be kind, be respectful, but you don't need that weight and negativity going into you.

And if you're in a work or school situation or if you live with someone who's a weight, don't let them steal your joy or sour you with their issues. Some people don't want to be happy. They're always in the pits. You've got to have the attitude: "If you don't want to be happy, that's fine, but you're not going to keep me from being happy." Take extra doses of praise, encouragement, and inspiration. Stay prayed up and filled up. Set some boundaries. Don't let them keep you from your destiny. It's time to break free.

Consider This

———•———

Identify the people in your life who are lifters and
thrusters—the ones who inspire and motivate you
to run your own race and fulfill your destiny.
What can you do to spend more time with them,
and can you identify other people or ministries
that might do the same?

....
....
....
....
....
....
....
....
....
....
....
....
....
....
....
....
....

What the Scriptures Say

Barnabas wanted to take John along, the John nicknamed Mark. But Paul wouldn't have him; he wasn't about to take along a quitter who, as soon as the going got tough, had jumped ship on them in Pamphylia.

Acts 15:37–38 MSG

I want you to put your foot down. Take a firm stand on these matters so that those who have put their trust in God will concentrate on the essentials that are good for everyone. Stay away from mindless, pointless quarreling over genealogies and fine print in the law code. That gets you nowhere. Warn a quarrelsome person once or twice, but then be done with him. It's obvious that such a person is out of line, rebellious against God. By persisting in divisiveness he cuts himself off.

Titus 3:8–11 MSG

Thoughts for Today

Keep away from people who try to belittle your ambition.
Small people always do that, but the really great make
you feel that you, too, can become great.

Mark Twain

Encouragement is the oxygen of the soul.

George M. Adams

By friendship you mean the greatest love, the greatest usefulness, the most open communication, the noblest sufferings, the
severest truth, the heartiest counsel, and the greatest union of
minds of which brave men and women are capable.

Jeremy Taylor

. . . .

. . . .

. . . .

. . . .

. . . .

. . . .

. . . .

. . . .

. . . .

. . . .

. . . .

. . . .

. . . .

A Prayer for Today

Father, thank You for the people You've brought into my life who inspire and motivate me, who lift me up and thrust me forward to becoming the person You want me to be. Help me as I consider the people with whom I am giving my time and energies and show me where I need to put up boundaries in my present relationships. I want to be loving and kind and helpful, but I refuse to carry others' weights and negativities. I am believing that You will open the door for more lifters and thrusters in my life to keep me running straight ahead.

. . . .

. . . .

. . . .

. . . .

. . . .

. . . .

. . . .

. . . .

. . . .

. . . .

. . . .

. . . .

. . . .

. . . .

. . . .

TAKEAWAY TRUTH

You need to be around lifters and thrusters—people who inspire you and motivate you. Find people who are going to lift you up, push you forward, encourage you, and inspire you. Find people who do their best to leave you better than you were before. Be secure enough in who you are that you don't live to please people who would drag you down. Be kind. Be compassionate, but run your own race.

EXPECT
GOOD
THINGS

CHAPTER 7
Upgrade Your Expectations

Key Truth

Our expectations set the limits for our lives. If you expect little, you're going to receive little. But if you expect more favor, good breaks, and promotions, you will see new levels of favor and success.

A young man told me: "I don't want to expect too much. That way if it doesn't happen, I won't go to bed all disappointed."

That's no way to live. If you're not expecting increase, promotion, or good breaks, you're not releasing your faith. Faith is what causes God to act. If you expect a break and it doesn't happen, don't go to bed disappointed. Go to bed knowing you're one day closer to seeing it come to pass. Get up the next morning and do it again.

Winners develop this third undeniable quality of expecting good things. You can't be in neutral and hope to reach your full potential or have God's best. It's not enough to not expect anything bad; you have to aggressively expect good things. Are you expecting your dreams to come to pass? Do you expect this year will be better than last year? Are you expecting to live a long, healthy, blessed life? Pay attention to what you're expecting.

Maybe you have a desire to get married. Don't go around thinking: "I'll never meet anyone. It's been so long, and I'm getting too old." Instead, expect to be at the right place at the right time. Believe that divine connections will come across your path. Believe that the right person will be attracted to you.

"What if I do that and nothing happens?"

What if you do it and something does happen? I can tell you nothing will happen if you don't believe.

David said in Psalm 23:6: "Surely your goodness and love will follow me all the days of my life." In the past you may have had disappointments and setbacks following you around, but you need to let go of what didn't work out. Let go of every mistake, and let go of every failure.

Expect goodness and mercy to follow you wherever you go. It's good to look back sometimes and just say, "Hey, goodness. Hey, mercy. How are you doing back there?"

Some people don't realize that they're always looking for the next disaster, looking for the next failure, or looking for the next bad break. Change what you're looking for. Start looking for goodness, mercy, favor, increase, and promotion. That's what should be following you around.

One definition of hope is "the happy anticipation of something good." If you're anticipating something good, it's going to bring you joy. It will give you enthusiasm. When you're expecting your dreams to come to pass, you'll go out each day with a spring in your step. But if you're not anticipating anything good, you'll drag through life with no passion. It's time to get your *expecter* out!

Consider This

Every morning when you wake up, do you declare,
"Something good is going to happen to me today"?
Through the day, do you have an attitude of
expectancy? Where can you start to upgrade
your expectations for today?

....
....
....
....
....
....
....
....
....
....
....
....
....
....
....
....
....
....

What the Scriptures Say

Surely, LORD, you bless the righteous; you surround
them with your favor as with a shield.

Psalm 5:12

I am the LORD your God, who brought you up out of Egypt.
Open wide your mouth and I will fill it.

Psalm 81:10

Thoughts for Today

Pray for great things, expect great things,
work for great things, but above all, pray.

R. A. Torrey

However many blessings we expect from God, His infinite
liberality will always exceed all our wishes and our thoughts.

John Calvin

I believe though I do not comprehend, and I hold
by faith what I cannot grasp with the mind.

Bernard of Clairvaux

....
....
....
....
....
....
....
....
....
....
....
....
....
....
....
....

A Prayer for Today

Father, I'm upgrading my expectations today and shaking off doubt, negativity, disappointments, self-pity, little dreams, and little goals. You are El Shaddai, the God Who is more than enough. This is my year to go to new levels of favor and success. I believe that You want to do something new, something amazing in my life. You are God, the God of the breakthrough who has first place in my life. I believe that You are about to do a new work in me, take me beyond the barriers of the past, and help me to step into the abundance You have in store.

TAKEAWAY TRUTH

If you raise your level of expectancy, God will take you places you've never dreamed. Expect breakthroughs. Expect problems to turn around. Expect to rise to new levels. You haven't seen your greatest victories. You haven't accomplished your greatest dreams. There are new mountains to climb, new horizons to explore. God will help you overcome obstacles that looked insurmountable, and you will see His goodness in amazing ways.

CHAPTER 8
Relive the Joy

Key Truth

When negative memories come up—the things that didn't work out, the hurts, and the disappointments—remember, that's not the only channel—get your remote control and switch over to the joy channel.

In the Old Testament, God commanded His people to have certain feasts and certain celebrations. One of the main reasons was so they would remember what He had done. Several times a year they were stop what they were doing so everybody could take off. They would celebrate how God brought them out of slavery and how God defeated their enemies and how He protected them. They were required to remember.

In another place it talks about how they put down what they called "memorial stones." These were big stones. Today, we would call them historical markers. The stones reminded them of specific victories. Every time they would go by certain stones they would recall an event. "This stone was for when we were brought out of slavery. This stone is for when our child was healed. This stone is for how God provided for our needs." Having these memorial stones helped them to keep God's deeds fresh in their memories.

In the same way, you should have your own memorial stones.

When you look back over your life, you should remember not when you failed, not when you went through a divorce, not when your business went down, not when you lost that loved one, not when the boss did you wrong. That's remembering what you're supposed to forget.

You need to switch over to the joy channel. Remember when you met the love of your life, remember when your child was born, remember when you received that new position, remember when the problem suddenly turned around, remember the peace you felt when you lost a loved one.

Remember the strength you had in that difficult time. It looked dark. You didn't think you'd see another happy day again, but God turned it around and gave you joy for mourning, beauty for ashes, and today you're happy, healthy, and strong. We should all have our own memorial stones.

If you'd just change what you're remembering—start remembering your successes, your victories, and the times you've overcome—that will allow you to step into new levels of favor. You may be in tough times, facing challenges, but when you remember the right things, you won't be saying, "This problem is too big. This sickness is going to be the end of me." Instead, you'll be saying, "God, You did it for me once, and I know You can do it for me again."

Instead of dwelling on how impossible it is and how you'll never make it, remember your victories all through the day. Get your memorial stones out. "Lord, thank You for that time when all the odds were against me, but You turned it around. God, I remember when You promoted me, vindicated me, and made my wrongs right."

Relive your victories and joys. Remembering the good things will make you strong.

Consider This

My mother recently marked the thirty-first
anniversary of her victory over cancer. Thirty-one
years ago, the doctors gave her a few weeks to live,
but another year just went by, and she's still healthy
and whole. That's a memorial stone. What memorial
stones do you need to remember in your life?

What the Scriptures Say

"Go over before the ark of the LORD your God into the middle of the Jordan. Each of you is to take up a stone on his shoulder, according to the number of the tribes of the Israelites, to serve as a sign among you. In the future, when your children ask you, 'What do these stones mean?' tell them that the flow of the Jordan was cut off before the ark of the covenant of the LORD. When it crossed the Jordan, the waters of the Jordan were cut off. These stones are to be a memorial to the people of Israel forever."

Joshua 4:5–7

I will tell of the kindnesses of the LORD, the deeds for which he is to be praised, according to all the LORD has done for us—yes, the many good things he has done for Israel, according to his compassion and many kindnesses.

Isaiah 63:7

....
....
....
....
....
....
....
....
....
....
....
....
....

Thoughts for Today

I know of nothing that so stimulates my faith in my Heavenly Father as to look back and reflect on His faithfulness to me in every crisis and every chilling circumstance of life. Over and over He has proved His care and concern for my welfare. Again and again I have been conscious of the Good Shepherd's guidance through dark days and deep valleys.

Phillip Keller

When we face difficulties, we sometimes forget God's past faithfulness. We see only the detours and the dangerous path. But look back and you will also see the joy of victory, the challenge of the climb, and the presence of your Traveling Companion who has promised never to leave you nor forsake you.

Author Unknown

....

....

....

....

....

....

....

....

....

....

....

....

....

....

A Prayer for Today

Father God, I am at peace today because I can look back
on the memorial stones in my life and remember with
joy the victories that You have accomplished. Thank You
for that time when all the odds were against me, but You
turned it around. I remember when You promoted me,
vindicated me, and made my wrongs right. I believe that
when negative memories come up that I have the power to
change to the joy channel and be strong in the
power of Your great might.

TAKEAWAY TRUTH

Quit focusing on what's wrong with
you and start focusing on what's right with
you. You won't ever become all you were
created to be if you're against yourself.
You have to retrain your mind. Be disciplined
about what you dwell on. Rehearse all the
times God has opened doors, given you
promotions, healed your family members,
and put you in the right places with the right
people. Don't forget your joys and victories.
On a regular basis go back over your memorial stones and relive the joy.

CHAPTER 9
God Can Do It Again

Key Truth

The key to staying encouraged so you can see God open new doors and turn negative situations around is to never forget what He has done. If you want to reach your Promised Land, look back and see the hand of God on your life.

God performed miracle after miracle for the Israelites. He sent plagues on their enemies and supernaturally brought them out of slavery. When they came to a dead end at the Red Sea, with Pharaoh and his army chasing them, it looked like their lives were all over, but the water parted and they went through the sea on dry ground. He led them by the cloud by day and the pillar of fire by night.

But in spite of all of this, they never made it into the Promised Land. Psalm 78 tells why. It says, "They forgot what God had done. They didn't remember the amazing miracles He had shown them and their ancestors."

Are you forgetting what God has done for you? Have you let what once was a miracle become ordinary? It doesn't excite you anymore. You don't thank God for it. Look back over your life and remember that God brought you to where you are, through big things and small things. You'll know that if God did it for you once, He can do it for you again.

You may get discouraged and think, "I don't see how I'll ever get out of this problem. I'll never get out of debt. I'll never get well." But when that negative thinking happens, go back and remember the Red Seas that God has parted for you. Remember the enemies He's delivered you from. Remember the battles He's fought, and the restoration, the vindication, and the favor He's shown.

Look back and see the hand of God on your life. He has opened doors that should have never opened for you and helped you accomplish things you never could have accomplished on your own. He's brought you out of difficulties that you thought you'd never survive. He's protected, promoted, and given you opportunity.

In the Old Testament, we read a lot about the staffs that people carried around with them. They weren't just walking sticks or something to keep wild animals away. They were more significant than that. They etched records of important events and dates on their walking staffs. Their walking staffs provided a record of their history with God.

When Moses parted the Red Sea, what did he do? He held up his staff. He was saying, "God, we thank You for all You've done in the past. We remember that You've delivered us time and time again." He was remembering the great things God had done.

When David went out to face Goliath, he didn't just take his slingshot. The Scripture says he took his staff. On that staff, no doubt, he had etched, "On this date I killed a lion with my bare hands. On this date I killed a bear." David took his staff to remind him that God had helped him in the past. That gave him the final boost. His attitude was, "God, You did it for me back then, so I know You can do it for me now."

Read the victories etched on your staff and go forth to conquer.

Consider This

The Scripture says, "We should never
forget what God has done in our lives, and we
should tell our children and our grandchildren."
We should pass down stories of the goodness of
God. If you had a staff, what victories would
you have etched on it that you should tell
your children and grandchildren?

What the Scriptures Say

———◆———

Hear this, . . . all who live in the land. Has anything like this ever happened in your days or in the days of your ancestors? Tell it to your children, and let your children tell it to their children, and their children to the next generation.

Joel 1:2–3

Then I thought, "To this I will appeal: the years when the Most High stretched out his right hand. I will remember the deeds of the LORD; yes, I will remember your miracles of long ago. I will consider all your works and meditate on all your mighty deeds."

Psalm 77:10–12

Thoughts for Today

Sometimes a person has to go back, really back—to have a sense, an understanding of all that's gone to make them— before they can go forward.

Paule Marshall

We have forgotten the gracious Hand that preserved us in peace and multiplied and enriched and strengthened us; and we have vainly imagined, in the deceitfulness of our hearts, that all these blessings were produced by some superior wisdom and virtue of our own.

Abraham Lincoln

....
....
....
....
....
....
....
....
....
....
....
....
....
....
....

A Prayer for Today

Father, thank You for all the amazing things You've done
in my life, for the victories You've helped me win, for the
restoration, the vindication, and the favor You've shown.
Help me to remember the doors You've opened for me and
for the times You've protected, promoted, and given me
opportunities. I believe that no matter what I face today
that You can do the miracles again for me now just as
You've done in the past.

....
....
....
....
....
....
....
....
....
....
....
....
....
....
....
....
....

TAKEAWAY TRUTH

Are you facing giants today? Does your problem look too big? Do your dreams seem impossible? You need to get your staff out. Instead of going around discouraged and thinking it's never going to work out, start dwelling on your victories. Start thinking about how you killed the lion and bear in your own life. Start remembering how far God has brought you.

HAVE A
POSITIVE
MIND-SET

CHAPTER 10
Set Your Mind to Positive

Key Truth

Your happiness is all about your attitude toward life. It's not your circumstances that keep you unhappy. It's how you respond to them. You're as happy as you want to be.

Every day we get to choose our attitudes. We can determine to be happy and look on the bright side—expecting good things and believing we will accomplish our dreams—or we can elect to be negative by focusing on our problems, dwelling on what didn't work out, and living worried and discouraged.

These are the choices we all can make. Nobody can force you to have a certain attitude. Life will go so much better if you simply decide to be positive. That is the fourth undeniable quality of a winner.

It's not your circumstances that make you negative; it's your attitude about those circumstances. You can take twenty positive people and twenty negative people and give them the exact same problem—put them on the same job, in the same family, and at the same house—and the twenty positive people will come out just as positive and happy, with great attitudes. The negative people will still be just as negative. They can have the same problems and same circumstances, but much different attitudes.

What's the difference? Positive people have made up their minds to enjoy life. They focus on the possibility, not the problem.

They're grateful for what they have, and they don't complain about what they don't have. Positive people know that God is in control, and that nothing happens without His permission. They choose to bloom where they are planted. They're not waiting to be happy when the situation changes. They're happy while God is changing the situation.

When you're positive, you're passing the test. You're saying, "God, I trust you. I know you're fighting my battles."

If you are not happy where you are, you won't get where you want to be. Don't wait for everything to change before you have a good attitude. If you have a good attitude now, God can change the situation.

Before you leave the house in the morning, you need to make up your mind to stay positive and enjoy the day no matter what comes your way. You have to decide ahead of time. That's what it says in Colossians 3:2, "Set your mind on the higher things and keep it set." The higher things are the positive things. Set your mind for victory and success. Have the attitude: "This is going to be a great day. God's favor is on my life. I'm excited about my future."

You are a child of the Most High God. You've been crowned with favor. You were never created to live an average, get-by, short-end-of-the-stick life. You were created to be the head and not the tail, to lend and not borrow, to reign in life as a king. You have royalty in your blood. Winning is in your DNA.

When your mind is set as positive, hopeful, and expecting good things, that's when you'll go places you've never dreamed. New doors will open. New opportunities and the right people will come across your path.

Consider This

One person gets up and says, "Good morning, Lord!" Another person gets up and says, "Oh Lord, it's morning." Which person are you? What "higher things" do you need to set your mind upon?

What the Scriptures Say

Rejoice in the Lord always. I will say it again: Rejoice! Let your gentleness be evident to all. The Lord is near. Do not be anxious about anything, but in every situation, by prayer and petition, with thanksgiving, present your requests to God. And the peace of God, which transcends all understanding, will guard your hearts and your minds in Christ Jesus.

Philippians 4:4–7

Though the fig tree does not bud and there are no grapes on the vines, though the olive crop fails and the fields produce no food, . . . yet I will rejoice in the LORD, I will be joyful in God my Savior. The Sovereign LORD is my strength; he makes my feet like the feet of a deer, he enables me to tread on the heights.

Habakkuk 3:17–19

Thoughts for Today

Words can never adequately convey the incredible impact of our attitude toward life. The longer I live the more convinced I become that life is 10 percent what happens to us and 90 percent how we respond to it.

Charles R. Swindoll

There is little difference in people, but that little difference makes a big difference. The little difference is attitude. The big difference is whether it is positive or negative.

Clement Stone

Two men looked through prison bars—
one saw mud, the other stars.

Author Unknown

A Prayer for Today

Father, thank You that because I am Your child, and You are the Most High God, You have crowned me with favor. I will not be limited by my circumstances—by how I was raised, my education or environment, or by what I've been in the past. I'm setting my mind on higher things, pressing forward and taking new ground, stretching my faith, believing for bigger things, expecting Your blessing in unprecedented ways. I believe that You are taking me places I've never dreamed, and I can't wait to see what You have for me in the future.

....
....
....
....
....
....
....
....
....
....
....
....
....
....
....

TAKEAWAY TRUTH

You are not a victim. You're a victor. You wouldn't have opposition if there were not something amazing in your future. Keep a smile on your face. Set the tone for victory, for success, for new levels. Stay positive. Stay hopeful. Enlarge your vision. Make room for God to do something new. You haven't touched the surface of what He has in store.

CHAPTER 11
Get Your Hopes Up

Key Truth

If God showed you all He has planned for you and all the doors He's going to open, you'd be so amazed, excited, and passionate that it would be easy to set your mind for victory.

I was talking to a reporter one time, and I could tell he didn't like the fact that my message is so positive and so hopeful. He asked what I would tell a person who had lost a job and was about to lose a home and had no place to go and all sorts of other problems.

I said, "First of all, I would encourage that person to find something to be grateful for, and secondly, I would encourage the person to expect new doors to open and to expect breakthroughs."

The Scripture says, "When darkness overtakes the righteous, light will come bursting in." When you don't see a way out, and it's dark, you're in prime position for God's favor to come bursting in.

The reporter said, "Wouldn't that be giving them false hope?"

Here's the alternative: I could tell them be negative, bitter, give up, complain, and be depressed. All that would do is make matters worse.

You may be in a difficult situation, but instead of being negative, just dig in your heels and say, "I refuse to live with a negative attitude. I'm not giving up on my dreams. I'm not living without passion or zeal. I may not see a way, but I know God has a way. It may be dark, but I'm expecting the light to come bursting in. I'm setting my mind for victory."

That's what allows God to work. It's not just mind over matter. It's not just having a positive attitude. It's your faith being released. When you believe, it gets God's attention. When you expect your dreams to come to pass, your health restored, and good breaks and divine connections coming your way, then the Creator of the universe goes to work.

You may have had a thousand bad breaks, but don't use that as an excuse to be negative. One good break can make up for all the bad breaks. One touch of God's favor can catapult you further than you ever imagined. You may feel like you're getting behind. You're not where you thought you would be in life. Don't worry; God knows how to make up for lost time. He knows how to accelerate things.

Now you've got to do your part. What's in your future is greater than anything you've seen in your past. We need to get rid of Murphy's Law and live by just the opposite. Your attitude should be: "If anything can go right today, it will go right and happen to me at the best time. Nothing will be as difficult as it looks. Nothing will take as long as it seems."

Why? You are highly favored. Almighty God is breathing in your direction. You've been anointed, equipped, and empowered.

Some may claim I'm just getting hopes up and trying to get people to be more positive. It's true, and here's why: God is a positive God. There is nothing negative about Him. If you're negative, sour, or pessimistic, you're going against the flow of God. Get your hopes up, and get in the flow!

Consider This

---•---

When you are positive, hopeful, and expecting good
things, you are in the jet stream of almighty God.
You will accomplish more, live happier, and see
increase and favor. In what areas of your life do you
need to get your hopes up?

....

....

....

....

....

....

....

....

....

....

....

....

....

....

....

....

....

....

....

....

What the Scriptures Say

I pray that your hearts will be flooded with light so that you can understand the confident hope he has given to those he called— his holy people who are his rich and glorious inheritance.

Ephesians 1:18 NLT

. . . but those who hope in the LORD will renew their strength. They will soar on wings like eagles; they will run and not grow weary, they will walk and not be faint.

Isaiah 40:31

Thoughts for Today

Despondency does not become a prince,
much less a Christian. Our God is "the God of hope";
and we should hope in Him. We should hope in His mercy,
in His patience, in His provision, in His plenteous redemption.
We should hope for light in darkness; for strength in weakness;
for direction in perplexity; for deliverance in danger;
for victory in conflict, and for triumph in death.

James Smith

Hope itself is like a star, not to be seen in the sunshine of
prosperity, but only to be discovered in the night of adversity.

Charles Spurgeon

Do not let your happiness depend on something you may
lose . . . only (upon) the Beloved who will never pass away.

C. S. Lewis

....

....

....

....

....

....

....

....

....

....

....

....

A Prayer for Today

Father, thank You for unveiling Your great heart of love
and grace that bring me hope. Thank You that when I
don't see the way out, and it's dark, that You come bursting in with light and direction. I release my faith that You,
the Creator of the universe, have highly favored me. I
believe that You are accelerating things in my life
and that I am in the divine flow.

....
....
....
....
....
....
....
....
....
....
....
....
....
....
....
....
....
....
....

TAKEAWAY TRUTH

Shake off a negative mentality. Shake off pessimism, discouragement, and self-pity. Get your fire back. Life is passing you by. You don't have time to waste being negative. You have a destiny to fulfill. You have an assignment to accomplish. God's favor is surrounding you like a shield. You can, you will!

CHAPTER 12
Freshen Up Your Attitude

Key Truth

The Scripture says, "Put on a fresh new attitude." Yesterday's attitude is not good enough for today. Every morning you have to consciously adopt a fresh attitude of expecting an abundance of favor.

A lot of people rely on yesterday's attitude, or last week's attitude, or last year's attitude. I've found yesterday's attitude is not good enough for today. Every morning you have to consciously adopt a fresh attitude by thinking thoughts such as: "I'm going to be happy today. I'm going to go with the flow and not get upset. God is in control. He's directing my steps. No obstacle is too big. No dream is too great. I am well able to do what I'm called to do."

This is what the Bible's Daniel did. The Scripture says he had an excellent spirit. He was a cut above. He stood out in the crowd. How did he do it? Every morning he got up early, opened his window, and thanked God for the day. He thanked God for His goodness and thanked Him that he was well able. He was putting on that fresh new attitude, setting his mind for victory.

Daniel was serving the king in a foreign land, when the king issued a decree that no one could pray to any God except the king's God. If they did, they would be thrown into a lions' den. That threat didn't stop Daniel. He kept praying to Jehovah.

Daniel's enemies told the king, who loved Daniel, but the king couldn't go back on his word. Daniel said, "Don't worry, King. I'll be fine. The God I serve is well able to deliver me."

That's what happens when you start the day off in faith, thinking positive thoughts on purpose. When you're in a difficult situation, you don't shrink back in fear with thoughts such as, "Why is this happening to me?" Instead, you rise up in faith and say, "My God is well able. I'm armed with strength for this battle. I can do all things through Christ. If God be for me, who dare be against me?"

The authorities threw Daniel into the lions' den. Everyone expected Daniel to be eaten in a few minutes. But when you have this attitude of faith, God will fight your battles for you. God sent an angel to close the mouths of the lions. The king got him out and said, "From now on we're going to all worship the God of Daniel, the true and living God."

It's interesting that the Scriptures say nothing negative about Daniel. He had experienced a long list of bad circumstances. He'd been mistreated and faced huge obstacles. But if you study his life, you'll find that he was always positive. He had an attitude of faith. He didn't make excuses or ask, "God, why is this happening to me?"

If you develop this positive mind-set, I believe and declare that you will accomplish more than you ever imagined. You will overcome obstacles that looked impossible, and you will become everything God has created you to be. You can, you will!

Consider This

If you go around with negative thoughts, they will
drain you of your faith, your energy, and your zeal.
It's just like a big vacuum pulling out all the good
things that God put in you. How's your attitude?
Where do you need to freshen it up?

....
....
....
....
....
....
....
....
....
....
....
....
....
....
....
....
....

What the Scriptures Say

I have strength for all things in Christ Who empowers me
[I am ready for anything and equal to anything through
Him Who infuses inner strength into me;
I am self-sufficient in Christ's sufficiency].

Philippians 4:13 AMP

"When you pass through the waters, I will be with you; and
when you pass through the rivers, they will not sweep over you.
When you walk through the fire, you will not be burned; the
flames will not set you ablaze. For I am the LORD your God,
the Holy One of Israel, your Savior . . ."

Isaiah 43:2–3

....
....
....
....
....
....
....
....
....
....
....
....
....
....
....

Thoughts for Today

The greatest discovery of my generation is that human beings
can alter their lives by altering their attitudes of mind.

William James

Things turn out best for the people who make
the best of the way things turn out.

John Wooden

Our attitudes control our lives and are a secret
power working twenty-four hours a day, for good or bad.
It is of paramount importance that we know how
to harness and control this great force.

Charles Simmons

. . . .

. . . .

. . . .

. . . .

. . . .

. . . .

. . . .

. . . .

. . . .

. . . .

. . . .

. . . .

. . . .

. . . .

A Prayer for Today

Father, thank You that I can do all things through Christ who infuses inner strength into me. You said I am more than a conqueror, a victor and not a victim. I know You are well able, bigger than my problem, greater than this sickness, and more powerful than any enemy. Thank You that today I can put on a fresh attitude that expects the abundance of Your favor. Thank You that You are fighting my battles and directing my steps. I believe that You will help me overcome every obstacle that looks impossible.

TAKEAWAY TRUTH

Especially in difficult times, make sure you put on a fresh new attitude. Do as Daniel did. Get up every morning and set your mind for victory and keep it set. When negative thoughts come, dismiss them and make a declaration like Daniel's: "My God is well able. He's done it for me in the past, and I know He'll do it for me again in the future."

COMMIT TO EXCELLENCE

CHAPTER 13
Exceed Expectations

Key Truth

When you're a person of excellence, your life gives praise to God. You do more than necessary. You don't just meet the minimum requirements; you go the extra mile.

We live in a society in which mediocrity is the norm. Many people do as little as they can to get by. They don't take pride in their work or in who they are. If somebody is watching, they perform one way, but when nobody is watching, they cut corners.

If you are not careful, you can be pulled into this same mentality where you think it's okay to show up late to work, to look less than your best, or to give less than your best. But God doesn't bless mediocrity. God blesses excellence. I have observed that the fifth undeniable quality of a winner is a commitment to excellence.

When you have a spirit of excellence, you do your best whether anyone is watching or not. You do what Jesus said, "If a soldier demands you carry his gear one mile, carry it two miles" (Matthew 5:41). You don't just meet the minimum requirements; you do more than you have to. Others may go around looking sloppy and cutting corners, slacking off at work, compromising in school, letting their lawns go, but here's the key: You are not everyone else. You are a cut above. You are called to excellence. God wants you to set the highest standard.

You should be the model employee for your company. Your boss and your supervisors should be able to say to the new hires, "Watch him. Learn from her. Pick up the same habits. Develop the same skills. This person is the cream of the crop, always on time, has a great attitude, and does more than what is required."

When you have an excellent spirit like that, your life gives praise to God and you will not only see promotion and increase but you are honoring God. That's one of the best witnesses you can have. Some people never go to church or read the Bible. Instead, they're reading your life. They're watching how you live. You're representing almighty God.

When you go to work, you should be so full of excellence that other people want what you have. Don't slack off and give a halfhearted effort. Give it your all. Do your job to the best of your ability. You produce more than you have to. You stay ten minutes late. You don't start shutting down thirty minutes before closing. You put in a full day.

Many people show up to work fifteen minutes late. They get some coffee, wander around the office, and finally sit down to work a half hour late. They'll waste another half hour making personal phone calls and surfing the Internet. Then they wonder why they aren't promoted. It's because God doesn't reward sloppiness. God rewards excellence.

When you do more than what's required, you will see God's goodness in new ways. You may be declaring favor and promotion over your life and that's all good, but it's only one part. The second part is making sure you get to work on time, do more than what's required, and do better this year than last year.

Consider This

———•———

In Genesis 24, Rebekah went way beyond the call of duty (check it out). As a result, she was chosen to marry Isaac, who came from the wealthiest family of that time. God rewards excellence. In what ways, whether at home or at work or with your family and friends, can you improve on your excellence and bring greater honor to God?

What the Scriptures Say

Whatever you do, work at it with all your heart,
as working for the Lord, not for human masters, since you know
that you will receive an inheritance from the Lord as a reward.
It is the Lord Christ you are serving.

Colossians 3:23–24

Whatever your hand finds to do, do it with all your might . . .

Ecclesiastes 9:10

....
....
....
....
....
....
....
....
....
....
....
....
....
....
....
....
....
....

Thoughts for Today

The only certain means of success is to render
more and better service than is expected of you,
no matter what your task may be.

Og Mandino

As God's fellow worker, [man] is to reflect God's creative
activity on Monday in the factory no less than on Sunday
when commemorating the day of rest and worship.

Carl F. H. Henry

The best medals are pinned on those who go
"beyond the call of duty."

Robert E. Lee

....
....
....
....
....
....
....
....
....
....
....
....
....
....

A Prayer for Today

Father, thank You for calling me to live a life that honors
You and for the privilege of representing You, the almighty
God, to my loved ones and friends, my coworkers and
neighbors and strangers. I want to be a person of excellence in everything I do, to go the second mile and always
be my best, and I want that excellence to flow out of my
heart of love for You. I believe that as I give it my all that I
will see Your goodness and favor in my life in new ways.

TAKEAWAY TRUTH

Jesus said, "Do more than is expected; carry it two miles." That's the attitude you need to have: "I'm not doing just what I have to. I'm not doing the minimum amount to keep my job. I'm a person of excellence. I go above and beyond what's asked of me. I do more than is expected."

CHAPTER 14
Strive for Excellence

 Key Truth

When you're an excellent person, you're always taking steps to improve. Favor and being excellent go hand in hand. Increase, promotion, and reaching your highest potential are all tied to a spirit of excellence.

Many people do not enjoy God's favor like they should, because they don't pass the small tests. Being excellent may not be some huge adjustment you need to make. It may mean just leaving ten minutes earlier so you can get to work on time, not complaining when you have to clean up, or not making personal phone calls on work time—just small things. These may not seem like a big deal, but the Scripture says, "It's the little foxes that spoil the vines."

A while back, I was in a store's parking lot, and it was very windy outside. When I opened my car door, several pieces of trash blew out and flew about twenty feet in different directions. I looked around and there were already all kinds of other trash in the parking lot. I was in a hurry. I almost convinced myself to let them go, but at the last moment I decided I was going to be a person of excellence and pick up my trash. I ended up running all over that parking lot.

My mind was saying, "What in the world am I doing out here? It doesn't matter—let the stuff go." When I finally picked up all of the scattered trash, I came back to my car. I had not realized it, but a couple was sitting in the car next to mine, watching the whole thing. The man rolled the window down and said, "Hey, Joel, we watch you on television each week."

Then the lady said something very interesting. "We were watching to see what you were going to do."

I thought, "Oh, thank You, Jesus."

Whether you realize it or not, people are watching you. We represent God, and He is not sloppy. God is not run-down. God is not second-class. He is an excellent God. Make sure you're representing God the right way, whether it's through your life, your house, your car, your clothes, your cubicle, or your office.

It doesn't mean you must have the best to represent Him, but looking your best and taking care of your possessions are part of this lifestyle. I'm not talking about spending a lot of money. Sometimes a can of paint, pulling some weeds, cleaning the carpet, or getting more organized can make all the difference in the world. Do what you can to represent God in an excellent way. If you don't take care of what God has given you, how can He bless you with more?

God made you as a person of excellence. Maybe all you've seen modeled is mediocrity or sloppiness—and maybe the people you work around are always late and undisciplined. But God is calling you to set a new standard. He wants to take you places higher than you've ever dreamed of, but you've got to do your part and stir up the excellence on the inside. Don't make excuses. Don't say, "This is the way I've always been." Take this challenge and come up to a higher level of excellence.

Consider This

God made you as a person of excellence, and He's
calling you to set a new standard of excellence in
your life. What specific ways do you need to stir up
the excellence inside of you to represent Him right?

What the Scriptures Say

"You are the light of the world. A town built on
a hill cannot be hidden. Neither do people light a lamp
and put it under a bowl. Instead they put it on its stand,
and it gives light to everyone in the house. In the same way,
let your light shine before others, that they may see your
good deeds and glorify your Father in heaven."

Matthew 5:14–16

"Do not despise these small beginnings,
for the LORD rejoices to see the work begin . . ."

Zechariah 4:10 NLT

Thoughts for Today

Make it a life rule to give your best to whatever passes
through your hands. Stamp it with your manhood.
Let superiority be your trademark.

Orison S. Marden

Find your place and hold it; find your work and do it.
And put everything you've got into it.

Edward Box

It is our best work that He wants, not the dregs of our
exhaustion. I think He must prefer quality to quantity.

George MacDonald

....

....

....

....

....

....

....

....

....

....

....

....

....

....

....

A Prayer for Today

Father, thank You that You have made me as a person of excellence and that You live in me. I want to represent You in the right way, through my life, my house, my car, my clothes, my workplace, and my relationships. I believe You are calling me to step up to a higher level of excellence. Help me have an excellent spirit and to bring glory to Your name in a way that I never have before.

TAKEAWAY TRUTH

God lives in you. You are the temple
of the Most High God. He made you as a
person of excellence. Whether you have
much or a little, whether it's old or new, take
pride in what God has given you. Have an
excellent spirit. Stand out in the crowd.
Take this challenge and come up to
a higher level of excellence.

CHAPTER 15
Distinguish Yourself

Key Truth

When you honor God, you don't compromise. You don't just go with the flow and do what everyone else is doing. You make the excellent choices that outclass those who don't honor God.

The Scripture says Daniel had an excellent spirit. As a teenager, he was brought out of Judah into Babylon. The king had all these young men in training and the best of them—the smartest, strongest, and most talented—would be chosen as the next leaders.

They had a certain diet for them to eat and certain programs for them to follow. But Daniel had made a vow to God to always honor Him. The Babylonians worshiped idols. Daniel was respectful, but he wouldn't eat the king's fancy foods. He didn't just go along with what everyone else was doing. He made the more excellent choice.

Daniel 6:3 says, "Daniel so distinguished himself by his exceptional qualities that the king planned to put him over the whole kingdom." Notice it doesn't say: "God distinguished him and he got promoted." It says Daniel distinguished himself. *The Message* translation says, "Daniel completely outclassed the others."

That's what happens when, number one, you honor God and, number two, you have an excellent spirit. You don't compromise. You don't just go with the flow and do what everyone else is doing.

Even if everyone else is late, everyone else cuts corners, and everyone else is undisciplined, you should do as Daniel did and go the extra mile. Make the choice to be excellent.

The Scripture goes on to say Daniel was far wiser than the other young men. Daniel 1:17 states that God gave Daniel "knowledge and understanding of all kinds of literature and learning. And Daniel could understand visions and dreams of all kinds." When you have an excellent spirit, God will give you unprecedented favor, creativity, and ideas so that, like Daniel, you will stand out in the crowd.

My question is: Are you distinguishing yourself and not waiting for God to do it? Are you going the extra mile? Are you doing more than you have to? Are you improving your skills?

Examine your life. We all have areas in which we can strive for excellence, whether it's how we treat people, how we present ourselves, or how we develop our skills. Don't let something small keep you from the big things God wants to do. You are called to be a cut above. You have excellence on the inside. It's who you are. Now do your part and be disciplined to bring out your excellence.

If you'll have this spirit of excellence, God will breathe in your direction and cause you to stand out. You'll look up and be more creative, more skilled, more talented, and wiser with more ideas. I believe and declare that like Daniel, you will outperform, you will outclass, and you will outshine, and God will promote you and set you in a place of honor. You can, you will.

Consider This

—————•—————

Are you distinguishing yourself, as Daniel did,
and not waiting for God to do it? In what areas
can you strive for excellence, whether it's how
you treat people, how you present yourself,
or how you develop your skills?

....
....
....
....
....
....
....
....
....
....
....
....
....
....
....
....
....
....

What the Scriptures Say

Ezra came up from Babylon. He was a teacher well versed in the Law of Moses, which the LORD, the God of Israel, had given. The king had granted him everything he asked, for the hand of the LORD his God was on him.

Ezra 7:6–7

But while Joseph was there in the prison, the LORD was with him; he showed him kindness and granted him favor in the eyes of the prison warden. So the warden put Joseph in charge of all those held in the prison, and he was made responsible for all that was done there. The warden paid no attention to anything under Joseph's care, because the LORD was with Joseph and gave him success in whatever he did.

Genesis 39:20–23

....

....

....

....

....

....

....

....

....

....

....

....

....

....

Thoughts for Today

When we do the best that we can, we never know what miracle is wrought in our life, or in the life of another.

Helen Keller

Genesis 1 logs God's commitment to excellence when it says, "God saw all that He had made, and it was very good." Christians should always do good work. Christians ought to be the *best* workers wherever they are. They ought to have the *best* attitude, the *best* integrity, and be the *best* in dependability.

Kent Hughes

....
....
....
....
....
....
....
....
....
....
....
....
....
....
....
....

A Prayer for Today

Father, thank You that You didn't make me to just go with the flow and do what everyone else is doing. Thank You that I can commit myself to striving for excellence, whether it's in how I treat people, how I present myself to others, or how I develop my skills. I believe that as I honor You with my choices that You will breathe in my direction and cause me to stand out and shine for Your glory.

TAKEAWAY TRUTH

You have excellence on the inside. It's who you are. Don't let something small keep you from the big things God wants to do. Do your part and be disciplined to bring out your excellence. God will breathe in your direction and cause you to stand out, outperform, outclass, and outshine those around you, and He will promote you and set you in a place of honor. You can, you will.

KEEP GROWING

CHAPTER 16
Grow Your Gifts

Key Truth

Winners don't coast through life relying on what they have already learned. You have treasure on the inside—gifts, talents, and potential—put in you by the Creator of the universe. But those gifts must be developed.

Too many people suffer from destination disease. They reach a certain level, earn their degrees, get a job, buy their home, and then just coast, thinking they're finished with their training.

However, winners never stop learning, and this is the sixth undeniable quality I have observed. God did not create us to reach one level and then stop. You should constantly be learning, improving your skills, and getting better at what you do.

You have to take responsibility for your own growth. Growth is not automatic. What steps are you taking to improve? Are you reading books or listening to educational videos or audios? Are you taking any courses on the Internet or going to seminars? Do you have mentors? Are you gleaning information from people who know more than you?

I read that the wealthiest places on earth are not the oil fields of the Middle East or the diamond mines of South Africa. The wealthiest places are the cemeteries. Buried in the ground are businesses that were never formed, books that were never written, songs that were never sung, dreams that never came to life, potential that was never released.

Don't go to your grave with that buried treasure. Keep growing. Keep learning. Every day we should have a goal to grow in some way, to learn something new.

There are all kinds of opportunities to increase. There is more knowledge available today than any time in history. You have no excuse for not improving. You don't have to go to the library. You don't even have to travel to a university. With the Internet, information flows right into your home. The Internet is for more than sharing pictures and playing games—it's a tool that can help you increase your gifts.

You have a responsibility not only to God, not only to your family, but also to yourself to develop what He's put in you. If you're in sales, human resources, auto mechanics, or health care, you can always expand your knowledge and improve your skills. Read books to learn how to communicate, work as a team member, or lead more effectively.

No matter what you do, there are people who have gone where you're going. Listen to what they have to say. Take twenty minutes a day, turn off the TV, and invest in yourself.

A lot of times we sit back and think, "God, I'm waiting on You. I'm waiting for that big break." Let me tell you who gets the big breaks—people who are prepared, those who develop their skills continuously. You've got to be proactive to take these steps to grow. When God sees you doing your part and developing what He's given you, then He'll do His part and open up doors that no man can shut.

Consider This

———•———

Where would you say that there is buried
treasure in your life that needs to be released?
What steps will you take to develop the potential
God has placed inside of you?

....

....

....

....

....

....

....

....

....

....

....

....

....

....

....

....

....

....

What the Scriptures Say

And Jesus grew in wisdom and stature,
and in favor with God and man.

Luke 2:52

Not that I have already obtained all this, or have
already arrived at my goal, but I press on to take hold
of that for which Christ Jesus took hold of me.

Philippians 3:12

Thoughts for Today

What is life all about? Development, growth. The two great laws of life are growth and decay. When things stop growing, they begin to die. This is true of men, business, or nations.

Charles Gow

The strongest principle of growth lies in human choice.

George Eliot

Life consists of melting illusions, correcting mistakes, and replacing outgrown clothing. But, I remind myself, there is no other way to grow.

A. P. Gouthey

....
....
....
....
....
....
....
....
....
....
....
....
....
....
....

A Prayer for Today

———•———

Father, thank You for the treasure You put inside of me—the gifts, the talents, and the potential—and all of the opportunities You provide for my growth. I don't want to coast through life relying on what I've already learned, but I want to do everything I can to develop the gifts and the potential. Help me to be doing something intentional and strategic every day to improve my skills. I believe that as I do that You will open up doors for me that no man can shut.

....
....
....
....
....
....
....
....
....
....
....
....
....
....
....
....

TAKEAWAY TRUTH

You should be doing something intentional and strategic every day to improve your skills. Don't be vague in your approach. Do not say things such as, "If I have time, I'll do it." You are better than that. You've got too much in you to stay where you are. Your destiny is too great to get stuck. Come up with a personal growth plan and start right now!

WHAT'S
YOUR
PLAN?

CHAPTER 17
Prepare Yourself to Be a Winner

Key Truth

The Scripture says, "A man's gift makes room for him." When God sees you prepare yourself, He opens new doors. If no new doors are opening, don't be discouraged. Just develop your gifts in a new way. Improve your skills.

Whether you are a teacher, a carpenter, a banker, or a doctor, don't settle where you are. Don't coast or rest on your laurels. Stir up what God has put in you and get better at it. There are new levels in your future. Things have shifted in your favor. God is looking for people who are prepared and taking steps to improve. He is looking for those who are serious about fulfilling their destinies.

Think about David in the Bible. He was out in the fields taking care of his father's sheep. In today's terms he had a boring minimum wage job and no friends, and it didn't look as though there was any opportunity for growth. He could have slacked off, been sloppy, unmotivated, and thought, "No reason to develop my skills. I have no opportunity. I'm stuck out here with these sheep."

Instead, while he was alone, he did not sit around bored and waste time. He practiced using his slingshot day after day and month after month. I can envision him setting up a target, slinging rocks again and again, learning, getting better, making adjustments, and sharpening his skills. He became a sharpshooter, a marksman, so precise, so skillful; he could hit a bull's-eye from a hundred meters away.

When God sought somebody to defeat a giant, somebody to lead His chosen people, He looked to see who was prepared. He wanted someone who had developed their skills, who had taken the time to cultivate the gifts He had put in them. He didn't choose just anybody—He selected a skilled marksman who could hit a target with precision.

In the same way, when God seeks somebody to promote, He doesn't just randomly close His eyes and say, "I'll pick this one. You won the lottery. It's your lucky day."

No, God looks for people who have developed their skills. When we read about David standing before Goliath and slinging that rock, sometimes we think it was all God's hand at work. In a sense it was God, but the truth is God didn't sling the rock. God didn't cause the rock to hit Goliath in just the right place.

It was David, who developed and used the skills God gave him. Like David, God has put in you a set of special skills that will slay giant challenges and open new doors—skills that will thrust you to new levels. But here's the key: Your skills have to be developed. Every day you spend learning, growing, and improving will prepare you for that new level.

I want to light a new fire under you. You need to kick it into a new gear. Produce more than you've been producing. Take some classes to increase your skills. Step it up a notch. Don't settle for a low position where no one will miss you. You have treasure in you. There is talent and skill that will cause you to be noticed. Proverbs 22:29 says, "Do you see a person skilled in their work? They will stand before kings and great men." Keep sharpening your skills. Cream always rises to the top.

Consider This

———•———

Despite being a slave and a prisoner, Joseph made himself so valuable that he kept rising to the top (Genesis 39). What steps will you take to better yourself so you are prepared to go to the next level?

What the Scriptures Say

"I am sending you Huram-Abi, a man of great skill . . . He is trained to work in gold and silver, bronze and iron, stone and wood, and with purple and blue and crimson yarn and fine linen. He is experienced in all kinds of engraving and can execute any design given to him. He will work with your skilled workers and with those of my lord, David your father."

2 Chronicles 2:13–14

Do your best to present yourself to God as one approved, a worker who does not need to be ashamed and who correctly handles the word of truth.

2 Timothy 2:15

....

....

....

....

....

....

....

....

....

....

....

....

....

....

....

Thoughts for Today

Everyone's got it in him, if he'll only make up his mind and stick at it. None of us is born with a stop-valve on his powers or with a set limit to his capacities. There's no limit possible to the expansion of each one of us.

Charles M. Schwab

The barriers are not erected that can say to aspiring talents and industry, "Thus far and no farther."

Ludwig van Beethoven

No matter what the level of your ability, you have more potential than you can ever develop in a lifetime.

James T. McCay

....
....
....
....
....
....
....
....
....
....
....
....
....
....
....

A Prayer for Today

Father, thank You that You have put in me a set of special skills that will slay giant challenges and open new doors for me—skills that will thrust me to new levels in my future. I want to kick it into a new gear and prepare myself and develop those skills so that I can fulfill my destiny. I believe that You will fill me with wisdom and use my gifts and strengths to bring great glory to Your name.

TAKEAWAY TRUTH

Don't come down with destination disease. Break out of that box and learn something new. Will Rogers said, "Even if you're on the right track, if you just sit there, eventually you're going to get run over." If you don't take steps to keep growing, then don't be surprised if someone comes along and takes the promotion that belongs to you.

CHAPTER 18
Surround Yourself with the Right People

Key Truth

Winners need to associate with inspiring people who build you up, people who challenge you to go higher, not anyone who pulls you down and convinces you to settle where you are.

If you want to keep growing, you need to have good mentors, people who have been where you want to go, people who know more than you. Let them speak into your life. Listen to their ideas. Learn from their mistakes. Study how they think and how they got to where they are.

I heard about a company that held a sales class for several hundred employees. The speaker asked if anyone knew the names of the top three salespeople. Every person raised a hand. He then asked how many of them had gone to lunch with these top salespeople and taken time to find out how they do what they do. Not one hand went up.

There are people all around us whom God put in our paths on purpose so we can gain wisdom, insight, and experience, but we have to be open to learning from them. Look around and find the winners you could learn from.

I say this respectfully: Don't waste your valuable time with people who aren't contributing to your growth. Life is too short to hang around people who are not going anywhere. Destination disease is contagious. If you're with them long enough, their lack of ambition and energy will rub off on you.

Who you associate with makes a difference in how far you go in life. If your friends are Larry, Curly, and Moe, you may have fun, but you may not be going anywhere.

The Scripture says, "We should redeem the time." You need to see time as a gift. God has given us 86,400 seconds each today. You're not being responsible with what God gave you if you're hanging out with time wasters who have no goals and no dreams.

You have a destiny to fulfill. God has amazing things in your future. It's critical that you surround yourself with the right people. If you're the smartest one in your group, then your group is too small. You need to be around people who know more than you and have more talent than you. Don't be intimidated by them; be inspired.

If you take an oak tree seed and plant it in a five-gallon pot, that tree will never grow to the size it was created to be. Why? It's restricted by the size of the pot. In the same way, God has created you to do great things. He's put talent, ability, and skills on the inside. You don't want to be restricted by your environment. It may be too small.

The people you hang around with may think small or be negative and drag you down. You need to get out of that little pot because God created you to soar. It's fine to help people in need, but don't spend all your time with them.

You need talented and smart people in your life; winners who are farther along than you and can inspire you and challenge you to rise higher.

Consider This

Have you surrounded yourself with the right people? Who are you learning wisdom, insight, and experience from? How can you expand your circle of those who inspire you to go to higher levels?

What the Scriptures Say

Whatever you have learned or received or heard from me,
or seen in me—put it into practice. And the God
of peace will be with you.

Philippians 4:9

Do not be so deceived and misled! Evil companionships
(communion, associations) corrupt and deprave good
manners and morals and character.

1 Corinthians 15:33 AMP

....
....
....
....
....
....
....
....
....
....
....
....
....
....
....
....
....
....

Thoughts for Today

Every man is like the company he is wont to keep.

Euripides

Your outlook upon life, your estimate of yourself,
and your estimate of your value are largely colored by your
environment. Your whole career will be modified, shaped,
molded by your surroundings, by the character of the
people with whom you come in contact every day.

Orison S. Marden

We begin to see the importance of selecting our
environment with the greatest of care, because environment
is the mental feeding ground out of which the food
that goes into our minds is extracted.

Napoleon Hill

. . . .
. . . .
. . . .
. . . .
. . . .
. . . .
. . . .
. . . .
. . . .
. . . .
. . . .

A Prayer for Today

Father, thank You that created me to do great things,
and You've put talent, ability, and skills on the inside that
are waiting to be developed. I don't want to be restricted
by my environment and associating with the wrong
people. Help me to redeem the time and give me the
wisdom to surround myself with inspiring people who
build me up and challenge me to rise higher.
I believe You have amazing things in my future.

....
....
....
....
....
....
....
....
....
....
....
....
....
....
....

TAKEAWAY TRUTH

When you take responsibility for your growth, God will honor your efforts. Promotion, good breaks, businesses, books, and divine connections are in your future. There is treasure in you, waiting to be developed. Redeem the time. Make a decision to surround yourself with the right people who know more than you and have more talent than you. Don't be intimidated by them; be inspired.

SERVE
OTHERS

CHAPTER 19
You Were Created to Serve

Key Truth

Jesus said, "If you want to be great in the kingdom, if you want to live a blessed life, there's a simple key: You have to serve other people."

M any people are not happy, because they are focused only on themselves. It's all about "my dreams, my goals, and my problems." That self-centered focus will limit you. You have to get your mind off of yourself.

You were created to give. Jesus said you were created to make the lives of others better. He wasn't talking about an event that happens every once in a while. He was talking about a lifestyle in which you live to help others, and you're always looking for ways to serve.

When you live a "serve others" lifestyle, you help friends, volunteer in your community, and take care of loved ones. It's not something you have to force yourself to do. It becomes a part of who you are. You develop an attitude of giving to everyone you meet. That's when you'll have true happiness and true fulfillment. You live not to receive, but to give.

God has put people in your life on purpose so you can be a blessing to them. Someone needs what you have. Someone needs your love. Someone needs your smile. Someone needs your encouragement and your gifts. Every morning you should ask,

"God, what is my assignment today? Help me to see the people You want me to be good to."

I've known my friend Johnny my whole life, more than forty years. He is constantly serving others. He's always running somebody to the airport, taking a friend to dinner, encouraging a pastor, or helping somebody on a project. When my father was on dialysis, if one of the family members couldn't take him to the clinic, we'd ask Johnny and he'd gladly do it.

I called Johnny one hot Saturday afternoon. When he answered the phone, it was very noisy in the background. I asked him where he was. He said, "I'm on top of a house. My friend's next door neighbor is an elderly lady, and we told her we'd reroof her house this weekend." He didn't even know the lady. She was just the neighbor of a friend. But Johnny has developed this mentality to serve others. When you serve others, you are serving God. When you do it for them, you're doing it for Him.

Jesus said, "If you give a cup of cold water to someone in need, you will surely be rewarded." Every time you serve, God sees it. Every time you help someone else. Every time you sacrifice—you go out of your way to pick up a friend, you get up early to sing in the choir, you stay late to help a coworker—God is keeping the record.

You don't need people's applause. You don't need anyone cheering you on. You don't need the Employee of the Month plaque; you are doing it unto God. He's the One who matters. He sees your acts of kindness. When you serve others, God says you'll be great in the kingdom.

Consider This

———— • ————

Would you say that you live a "serve others" lifestyle? What might you do to develop more of an attitude of giving to everyone you meet?

....
....
....
....
....
....
....
....
....
....
....
....
....
....
....
....
....
....

What the Scriptures Say

Each of you should use whatever gift you have received to serve others, as faithful stewards of God's grace in its various forms.

1 Peter 4:10

"Whoever wants to become great among you must be your servant, and whoever wants to be first must be your slave— just as the Son of Man did not come to be served, but to serve, and to give his life as a ransom for many."

Matthew 20:26–28

....
....
....
....
....
....
....
....
....
....
....
....
....
....
....
....
....
....
....

Thoughts for Today

Do all the good you can, by all the means you can, in all the ways you can, in all the places you can, at all the times you can, to all the people you can and as long as you can.

John Wesley

I do not believe one can settle how much we ought to give. I am afraid the only safe rule is to give more than we can spare.

C. S. Lewis

I used to ask God to help me. Then I asked if I might help Him. I ended up by asking Him to do His work through me.

Hudson Taylor

....
....
....
....
....
....
....
....
....
....
....
....
....
....
....

A Prayer for Today

———◆———

Father, thank You that You created me to serve others,
to be blessed by giving to others, to be truly fulfilled by
making the lives of others better. God, what is my
assignment today? Help me to see the people You want
me to be good to, the ones who need what I have, and the
ones who need my love and encouragement. I don't need
the applause of others, but I'm thrilled to know that as
I give, You keep a record of it. I would love to be
great in and for Your kingdom!

. . . .

. . . .

. . . .

. . . .

. . . .

. . . .

. . . .

. . . .

. . . .

. . . .

. . . .

. . . .

. . . .

. . . .

. . . .

TAKEAWAY TRUTH

If you want a great life, it doesn't just come from success, having a bigger house, or more accomplishments. There's nothing wrong with those things. God wants you to be blessed. But if you want to truly be fulfilled, you have to develop the habit of serving others.

CHAPTER 20
Lift Others and God Will Lift You

Key Truth

When you serve others, there will be a satisfaction that money can't buy. You'll feel a peace, a joy, a strength, and a fulfillment that only God can give.

Jesus and the disciples had traveled a long way to Samaria and were tired and hungry. He sent the disciples into town to get food while He waited at a well. There He met a woman. He told her about her future and gave her life a whole new beginning (John 4).

When the disciples arrived with the food, they were surprised that Jesus wasn't hungry or tired anymore. He was sitting by the well satisfied, at peace, and wouldn't take the food they offered. He said, "I have food that you know nothing about." They thought maybe somebody came while they were gone and gave Him something to eat. They talked about it: "He was tired a minute ago; now He's refreshed. He was hungry, but now He says He's satisfied. How could that be?"

Jesus overheard them trying to figure it out. He told them the secret. He said, "My meat is to do the will of Him that sent me, to accomplish His work." He was saying, "I get fed by doing what God wants me to do. I get nourished when I help people. My food, strength, peace, joy, and satisfaction come when I serve others."

When you do the will of your Father, it doesn't drain you; it replenishes you. You may volunteer in your community each week. You may get up early and go to church on your day off, maybe serving in the children's ministry after working all week. You may clean houses in the Saturday morning community outreach. You may spend the afternoon at the prison encouraging the inmates. You'd think you would leave tired, worn out, run-down, and needing to go home and rest after volunteering all day. But just like with Jesus, when you help others, you get fed.

Strength, joy, energy, peace, wisdom, and healing come to those who serve. You should be run-down, but God reenergizes and refreshes you so that at the end of the day you aren't down, you are up. You don't leave low, you leave high. God pays you back.

Jesus Christ modeled a servant attitude that overflowed with joy. He had all the power in the world. He was the most influential man who ever lived. Yet He bowed down and washed His disciples' feet. He could have hired someone to do it. He could have asked any of the disciples and they would have done it. He could have called an angel down from heaven and said, "Hey, do me a favor. Wash their feet. They stink. Peter needs some Odor Eaters! I don't want to deal with it today."

Instead, Jesus pulled out His towel, bowed down, and washed their feet one by one. He gave us His example of service to others so we would know you're never too important to be good to people. You are never too successful. You are never too high to bow down low and serve another person. The more you walk in humility, and the more willing you are to serve others, the higher God can take you. As you lift others, God will lift you.

Consider This

Who are you serving? Who are you being good to?
Who are you lifting up? Starting with your family,
how can you more effectively serve the people
God has brought into your life?

What the Scriptures Say

Serve one another humbly in love. For the entire law is fulfilled in keeping this one command: "Love your neighbor as yourself."

Galatians 5:13–14

Think of yourselves the way Christ Jesus thought of himself. He had equal status with God but didn't think so much of himself that he had to cling to the advantages of that status no matter what. Not at all. When the time came, he set aside the privileges of deity and took on the status of a slave, became *human*! Having become human, he stayed human. It was an incredibly humbling process. He didn't claim special privileges. Instead, he lived a selfless, obedient life and then died a selfless, obedient death—and the worst kind of death at that—a crucifixion.

Philippians 2:5–8 MSG

....
....
....
....
....
....
....
....
....
....
....
....
....

Thoughts for Today

———◆———

Trying to do the Lord's work in your own strength
is the most confusing, exhausting, and tedious of all work.
But when you are filled with the Holy Spirit, then
the ministry of Jesus just flows out of you.

Corrie ten Boom

We may easily be too big for God to use, but never too small.

D. L. Moody

Don't assume you have to be extraordinary to be
used by God. You don't have to have exceptional gifts,
talents, abilities, or connections. God specializes in using
ordinary people whose limitations and weaknesses make them
ideal showcases for His greatness and glory.

Nancy Leigh DeMoss

....

....

....

....

....

....

....

....

....

....

....

....

A Prayer for Today

Father, thank You that Your Son Jesus, who
had all of the power and authority in the world, modeled
a servant attitude that overflowed with joy. Thank You for
the strength, joy, energy, peace, wisdom, and healing that
come when I humble myself and serve others. All through
the day help me to speak kind words, offer compliments,
give encouragement, and lift up those around me.
I believe that as I lift others, You will lift me.

TAKEAWAY TRUTH

Be on the lookout for others whom you can bless. God puts people in our lives on purpose so we can brighten their days. You should get up every morning and say, "God, show me my assignment today. Help me to be sensitive to the needs of those around me." The Scripture says, "A kind word works wonders." All through the day we can serve God by speaking kind words, offering compliments, giving encouragement, and lifting up those around us.

CHAPTER 21
You Will Be Rewarded

Key Truth

God sees every act of service and kindness. He sees every good deed. Nothing you've done has gone unnoticed. God saw it, and the good news is you will be rewarded.

On a Saturday service awhile ago, I was baptizing people, and among them was an older man who'd had a stroke. He was in a wheelchair and couldn't walk at all. The younger man pushing him in the wheelchair was about my age. You could tell that he really cared about the man. He went to great lengths to make sure he was okay.

To get in the church baptistery, you have to go up some stairs and then walk down stairs into the water. A couple of men helped the older man stand up. Then the younger man put his arms under his legs and his back so he could carry the elderly man into the water, just like you'd carry a sleeping baby. It was a very moving scene, watching the younger man help someone so determined to be baptized despite his age and disabilities.

With the young man's help, we were able to baptize the elderly man. After we returned him to his wheelchair, I asked the younger man: "Is that your father?"

He shook his head no.

"Is he your uncle or your relative?" I asked.

The younger man explained that they'd just met in church a few weeks earlier. He said that on the Sunday I announced the baptism date, the older man in the wheelchair turned to him and said, "I wish I could be baptized. I always wanted to, but I had this stroke. I knew I should have done it sooner."

The young man offered to help him. The elderly man said he didn't have any family to bring him to church. The young man said, "Don't worry. I'll take care of you." He picked up the stranger at his home, helped him get to the baptism at our church, and carried him in and out of the baptistery. They'd only met once before in church.

My prayer is "God help us all to have that same compassion. Help us not to be so busy, so caught up in our own lives that we miss opportunities to serve others." God asks us to carry others in need. Maybe you won't have to carry them physically, but instead just lighten their loads. Will you help bring their dreams to pass? Will you go out of your way to be good to them?

Helping less fortunate people is the closest thing to the heart of God. I will never forget the image of that young man carrying the disabled man into the water. Jesus said, "When you do it to the least of these, you're doing it unto Me." I love the fact this young man wasn't looking for credit. He didn't have anyone cheering for him. He was just quietly serving this man.

Remember that when you are good to others and go out of your way to be a blessing—or when you make sacrifices no one knows about—God sees what you are doing. He sees your heart of compassion. Maybe no one else on this earth is singing your praises, but up there all of heaven is cheering you on.

Consider This

How can you help bring others' dreams to pass?
How can you go out of your way to be good to
them? What can you do to make a real
difference in someone's life?

....
....
....
....
....
....
....
....
....
....
....
....
....
....
....
....
....
....

What the Scriptures Say

"Truly I tell you, anyone who gives you a cup of water
in my name because you belong to the Messiah
will certainly not lose their reward."

Mark 9:41

"Be careful not to practice your righteousness in front of others
to be seen by them. If you do, you will have no reward from
your Father in heaven. So when you give to the needy, do not
announce it with trumpets, as the hypocrites do in the syna-
gogues and on the streets, to be honored by others. Truly I tell
you, they have received their reward in full. But when you give to
the needy, do not let your left hand know what your right hand
is doing, so that your giving may be in secret. Then your Father,
who sees what is done in secret, will reward you."

Matthew 6:1–4

Thoughts for Today

Nothing is ever wasted in the kingdom of God.
Not one tear, not all our pain, not the unanswered question
or the seemingly unanswered prayers. Nothing will be wasted
if we give our lives to God. And if we are willing to be patient
until the grace of God is made manifest, whether it takes
nine years or ninety, it will be worth the wait.

Author Unknown

Come work for the Lord. The work is hard,
the hours are long, and the pay is low, but the retirement
benefits are out of this world.

Author Unknown

What we weave in life will be worn in eternity.

Author Unknown

A Prayer for Today

Father God, help me to have the same heart of compassion
as the young man who helped the man with the stroke.
Help me not to be so busy, so caught up in my own life
that I miss opportunities to serve others. I want to do the
things that are on Your heart for others. I believe that as I
do, I am doing it for You as well, and I am delighted that
the day will come when You reward me for it.

TAKEAWAY TRUTH

Be on the lookout for ways you can be good to people. If you develop a lifestyle of serving others, God promises you will be great in the kingdom. I believe and declare because you're a giver, you will come in to your reward. You will come in to health, strength, opportunity, promotion, and breakthroughs.

►►► **SECTION VIII**

STAY
PASSIONATE

CHAPTER 22
Live in Amazement

Key Truth

Paul told Timothy in the Bible: "Stir up the gift, fan the flame." When you stir up the passion, your faith will allow God to do amazing things.

Studies show that enthusiastic people get better breaks. They're promoted more often, have higher incomes, and live happier lives. That's not a coincidence. The word *enthusiasm* comes from the Greek word *entheos*. *Theos* is a term for "God."

When you're enthusiastic, you are full of God. When you get up in the morning excited about life, recognizing that each day is a gift, you are motivated to pursue your goals. You will have a favor and blessing that will cause you to succeed.

The eighth undeniable quality of a winner is that they stay passionate throughout their lives. Too many people have lost their enthusiasm. At one time they were excited about their futures and passionate about their dreams, but along the way they hit some setbacks. They didn't get the promotions they wanted, maybe a relationship didn't work out, or they had health issues. Something took the wind out of their sails. They're just going through the motions of life; getting up, going to work, and coming home.

God didn't breathe His life into us so we would drag through the day. He didn't create us in His image, crown us with His favor, and equip us with His power so that we would have no enthusiasm.

You may have had some setbacks. The wind may have been taken out of your sails, but this is a new day. God is breathing new life into you. If you shake off the blahs and get your passion back, the winds will start blowing once again—not against you, but for you. When you get in agreement with God, He will cause things to shift in your favor.

My question for you is this: Are you really alive? Are you passionate about your life or are you stuck in a rut, letting the pressures of life weigh you down, or taking for granted what you have? You weren't created to simply exist, to endure, or to go through the motions; you were created to be really alive.

You have seeds of greatness on the inside. There's something more for you to accomplish. The day you quit being excited about your future is the day you quit living. When you quit being passionate about your future, you go from living to merely existing.

We all have seen God's goodness in some way. God opened a door, gave you a promotion, protected you on the freeway, and caused you to meet someone who has been a blessing. It was His hand of favor. Don't let it become ordinary. We should live in amazement at what God has done.

What has God done for you? Do you have healthy children? Do you have people to love? Do you have a place to work? Do you realize your gifts and talents come from God? Do you recognize what seemed like a lucky break was God directing your steps?

There are miracles all around us. Don't take them for granted. Don't lose the amazement of God's works. Fan your flames. Stir up your gifts.

Consider This

Recount some of the ways have you seen God's goodness in your life? What does that stir up within you about your future?

....
....
....
....
....
....
....
....
....
....
....
....
....
....
....
....
....

What the Scriptures Say

I will give thanks to you, Lord, with all my heart;
I will tell of all your wonderful deeds.

Psalm 9:1

Remember the wonders he has done, his miracles, and the
judgments he pronounced, you his servants, the descendants
of Israel, his chosen ones, the children of Jacob.

1 Chronicles 16:12–13

....
....
....
....
....
....
....
....
....
....
....
....
....
....
....
....
....
....

Thoughts for Today

Enthusiasm is the divine particle in our composition:
with it we are great, generous, and true; without it,
we are little, false, and mean.

L. E. Landon

Give me the love that leads the way, the faith that
nothing can dismay, the hope no disappointments tire,
the passion that will burn like fire; let me not sink to
be a clod: make me Thy fuel, Flame of God.

Amy Carmichael

God, I pray Thee, light these idle sticks of my life, that I may
burn for Thee. Consume my life, my God, for it is Thine. I
seek not a long life, but a full one, like You, Lord Jesus.

Jim Elliot

....

....

....

....

....

....

....

....

....

....

....

....

....

A Prayer for Today

Father God, You didn't breathe Your life into me so I would drag through the day. You didn't create me in Your image, crown me with Your favor, and equip me with Your power so that I would have no enthusiasm. I have recounted Your goodness in my life, the amazing things You have done, and I believe that You are breathing new life into me at this very moment. I'm shaking off the blahs, fanning the flames, and stirring up my gift, and I believe You are restoring my passion.

....
....
....
....
....
....
....
....
....
....
....
....
....
....

TAKEAWAY TRUTH

You may have had some setbacks. The wind may have been taken out of your sails, but this is a new day. God is breathing new life into you. If you shake off the blahs and get your passion back, the winds will start blowing once again—not against you, but for you. When you get in agreement with God, He will cause things to shift in your favor.

CHAPTER 23
Get in Agreement with God

Key Truth

God will complete what He started in your life. The Scripture says God will bring us to a flourishing finish. Get in agreement with God and stay passionate.

In the Bible, David said, "Lift up your head and the King of glory will come in." As long as your head is down and you are discouraged, with no joy, no passion, and no zeal, the King of glory will not come.

Instead, get up in the morning and say, "Father, thank You for another sunrise. I'm excited about this day." When you're really alive, hopeful, grateful, passionate, and productive, then the King of glory, the Most High God, will come in. He'll make a way where it looks like there is no way.

It's tempting to go through life looking in the rearview mirror. When you are always looking back, you become focused on what didn't work out, on who hurt you, and on the mistakes you've made, such as:

"If only I would have finished college."

"If only I'd spent more time with my children."

"If only I'd been raised in a better environment."

As long as you're living in regret, focused on the negative things of the past, you won't move ahead to the bright future God has in store. You need to let go of what didn't work out. Let go of your hurts and pains. Let go of your mistakes and failures.

You can't do anything about the past, but you can do something about right now. Whether it happened twenty minutes ago or twenty years ago, let go of the hurts and failures and move forward. If you keep bringing the negative baggage from yesterday into today, your future will be poisoned.

You can't change what's happened to you. You may have had an unfair past, but you don't have to have an unfair future. You may have had a rough start, but it's not how you start, it's how you finish.

Don't let a hurtful relationship sour your life. Don't let a bad break, a betrayal, a divorce, or a bad childhood cause you to settle for less in life. Move forward and God will pay you back.

Move forward and God will vindicate you. Move forward and you'll come into a new beginning. Nothing that's happened to you is a surprise to God. The loss of a loved one didn't catch God off guard. God's plan for your life did not end just because your business didn't make it, or a relationship failed, or you had a difficult child.

Here's the question: Will you become stuck and bitter, fall into self-pity, blame others, and let the past poison your future? Or will you shake it off and move forward, knowing your best days are still ahead?

The next time you are in your car, notice that there's a big windshield in the front and a very small rearview mirror. The reason the front windshield is so big and the rearview mirror is so small is that what's happened in the past is not nearly as important as what is in your future. Where you're going is a lot more important than where you've been.

Consider This

What negative baggage from the past do you need
to get rid of in order to move forward into the
fullness of God's future for you?

....
....
....
....
....
....
....
....
....
....
....
....
....
....
....
....
....
....

What the Scriptures Say

But one thing I do: Forgetting what is behind and straining toward what is ahead, I press on toward the goal to win the prize for which God has called me heavenward in Christ Jesus.

Philippians 3:13–14

There has never been the slightest doubt in my mind that the God who started this great work in you would keep at it and bring it to a flourishing finish on the very day Christ Jesus appears.

Philippians 1:6 MSG

Thoughts for Today

Why believe the devil instead of believing God? Rise
up and realize the truth about yourself—that all the past has
gone, and you are one with Christ, and all your sins have been
blotted out once and forever. O let us remember that it is sin
to doubt God's Word. It is sin to allow the past, which
God has dealt with, to rob us of our joy and our
usefulness in the present and in the future.

Martyn Lloyd-Jones

Be not the slave of your own past.

Ralph Waldo Emerson

Every experience God gives us, every person
He puts in our lives, is the perfect preparation for
the future that only He can see.

Corrie ten Boom

....

....

....

....

....

....

....

....

....

....

....

A Prayer for Today

Father God, thank You that I can lift up my
head and You, the King of glory, the Most High God,
will come in. I'm excited about this day. I agree with You
that I need to let go of past regrets, hurts, and pains that I
can't do anything about today. This is it. I'm letting go of
the past and moving forward with my life. I believe that
You will vindicate me with new beginnings and that
my best days are still ahead.

....

....

....

....

....

....

....

....

....

....

....

....

....

....

....

....

TAKEAWAY TRUTH

At the start of the day, forgive those who hurt you and let go of the setbacks and the disappointments from yesterday. God did not create you to carry around all that baggage. You may have been holding on to it for years. Put your foot down and say, "That's it. I'm not living in regrets and disappointments and dwelling on relationships that didn't work out, or on those who hurt me, or how unfairly I was treated. I'm letting go of the past and moving forward with my life."

CHAPTER 24
Get Ready for the New

Key Truth

Don't settle where you are. You can accomplish your dreams. Get ready for God's goodness. Get ready for God's favor. Get ready for the fullness of your destiny.

Pastor Dutch Sheets told a story about a forty-year-old lady having open-heart bypass surgery. Although this is a delicate procedure, it's performed successfully more than 230,000 times every year. During the operation, the surgeon clamped off the main vein flowing to the heart and hooked it to a machine that pumps the blood and keeps the lungs working. The heart actually stops beating while the vein is being bypassed.

When the procedure is over and the machine is removed, the warmth from the body's blood normally causes the heart to wake back up and start beating again. If that doesn't work, they have drugs that will wake up the heart.

This lady was on the operating table and the bypass was finished, so they let her blood start flowing, but for some reason her heart did not start beating. They gave her the usual drugs with no success. She had no heartbeat. The surgeon massaged her heart with his hand to stimulate that muscle and get it beating again, but even that did not work.

The surgeon was so frustrated, so troubled. It looked as if his patient was finished. After doing everything he could medically, he leaned over and whispered in her ear, "Mary, I've done everything I can do. Now I need you to tell your heart to beat again." He stepped back and heard *bump, bump, bump.* Her heart kicked in and started beating.

Do you need to tell your heart to beat again? Maybe you've been through disappointments and life didn't turn out like you had hoped. Now you're just sitting on the sideline. You've got to get your passion back. Get your fire back. Tell your heart to dream again. Tell your heart to love again. Tell your heart to laugh again.

Jesus said in Revelation 2, "I have one thing against you; you have left your first love." The scripture doesn't say you've lost your love; the passage says you've left your first love. That means you can go get it. You haven't lost your passion. You just left it. Go get it.

You haven't lost the love for your family; you've just left it—now go get it. You haven't lost that dream; it's still there in you. You just left it. You have to go get it.

You may have had some setbacks, but this is a new day. Dreams are coming back to life. Your vision is being renewed. Your passion is being restored. Hearts are beating again. Get ready for God's goodness. Get ready for God's favor.

Winning is in your DNA. The Most High God breathed His life into you. You've got what it takes. This is your time. This is your moment. Shake off doubts, shake off fear and insecurity, and get ready for favor, get ready for increase, get ready for the fullness of your destiny. You can, you will!

Consider This

———— • ————

What are the truths that you need to speak to your
own heart to get it beating again where you've
left a dream or a passion behind?

What the Scriptures Say

———— ✦ ————

Then he said to me, "Speak a prophetic message to these bones and say, 'Dry bones, listen to the word of the LORD! This is what the Sovereign LORD says: Look! I am going to put breath into you and make you live again! I will put flesh and muscles on you and cover you with skin. I will put breath into you, and you will come to life. Then you will know that I am the LORD.'"

Ezekiel 37:4–6 NLT

"So you'll go out in joy, you'll be led into a whole and complete life. The mountains and hills will lead the parade, bursting with song. All the trees of the forest will join the procession, exuberant with applause. No more thistles, but giant sequoias, no more thornbushes, but stately pines—monuments to me, to GOD, living and lasting evidence of GOD."

Isaiah 55:12–13 MSG

....

....

....

....

....

....

....

....

....

....

....

....

Thoughts for Today

The God who made us also can remake us.

Woodrow Kroll

By reading the Scriptures I am so renewed that
all nature seems renewed around me and with me.
The sky seems to be a pure, a cooler blue, the trees a deeper
green. The whole world is charged with the glory of God,
and I feel fire and music under my feet.

Thomas Merton

It is too late to mend the days that are past. The future
is in our power. Let us, then, each morning, resolve to send
the day into eternity in such a garb as we shall wish it to
wear forever. And at night let us reflect that one more
day is irrevocably gone, indelibly marked.

Adoniram Judson

. . . .
. . . .
. . . .
. . . .
. . . .
. . . .
. . . .
. . . .
. . . .
. . . .
. . . .
. . . .

A Prayer for Today

———•———

Father, thank You that You give me the power to speak to my heart and get back whatever good things I may have left behind in the past. Thank You that this is a new day and my dreams and vision and passions are being renewed by the power of Your Holy Spirit. I am ready for Your goodness and Your favor. I believe that I will see increase and the fullness of the destiny You created for me.

TAKEAWAY TRUTH

You have seeds of greatness on the inside.

Put these principles into action each day.

Get up in the morning expecting good

things. Go through the day positive, focused

on your vision, running your race, knowing

that you are well able. Not only are you able,

but I also declare you will become all

God created you to be. You can, you will!

A Final Word

Key Truth

God doesn't want you to be an imitation of someone else. You should be the original you were created to be. There is an anointing on your life, an empowerment, not to be somebody else, but to be you.

The Scripture says God has given us the power to enjoy what's appointed and allotted to us, which means I don't have the power to enjoy your life. You may have more money, more gifts, more friends, and a better job. But if you put me in your life, I will not enjoy it.

You are uniquely created to run your own race. Quit wishing you were someone else or thinking things such as, "If I had his talent . . ." If God wanted you to have his talent, He would give it to you. Take what you have and develop it. Make the most of your gifts.

Instead of thinking things such as, "If I had her looks . . . ," be grateful for the looks God gave you. That's not an accident. The life you have is perfectly matched for you.

Why don't you get excited about your life? Be excited about your looks, your talent, and your personality. When you are passionate about who you are, you bring honor to God. That's when

God will breathe in your direction, and the seeds of greatness He's planted on the inside will spring forth.

Really, it's an insult to God to wish you were someone else. You are saying, "God, why did You make me subpar? Why did You make me less than others?"

God didn't make anyone inferior. He didn't create anyone to be second-class. You are a masterpiece. You are fully loaded and totally equipped for the race that's designed for you.

Your attitude should be: "I may not be as tall, as tan, or as talented as someone else, but that's okay. Nobody will ever be a better me. I'm anointed to be me. I'm equipped to be me. And not only that, it's also easy to be me. It's easy to run my race because I'm equipped for what I need."

STAY**CONNECTED,**
BE**BLESSED.**

From thoughtful articles to powerful blogs, podcasts and more, JoelOsteen.com is full of inspirations that will give you encouragement and confidence in your daily life.

AVAILABLE ON JOELOSTEEN.COM

This daily devotional from Joel and Victoria will help you grow in your relationship with the Lord and equip you to be everything God intends you to be.

 **Joel Osteen STREAMING**

Miss a broadcast? Watch Joel Osteen on demand, and see Joel LIVE on Sundays.

 **Joel Osteen PODCAST**

The podcast is a great way to listen to Joel where you want, when you want.

CONNECT WITH US

PUT JOEL IN YOUR POCKET

Join our community of believers on your favorite social network.

Get the inspiration and encouragement of Joel Osteen on your iPhone, iPad or Android device! Our app puts Joel's messages, devotions and more at your fingertips.

Thanks for helping us make a difference in the lives of millions around the world.